OWNING THE U

T0013822

OWNING THE UNKNOWN

A Science Fiction Writer Explores
Atheism, Agnosticism, and the Idea of God

Robert Charles Wilson

Pitchstone Publishing
Durham, North Carolina

Pitchstone Publishing
Durham, North Carolina
www.pitchstonebooks.com

Copyright © 2023 by Robert Charles Wilson

"The Observer" was first published in the anthology *The UFO Files* (1998) and "In the Body of the Sky" was first published in the Canadian literary magazine *subTerrain* (2020).

All rights reserved.
Printed in the United States of America
First edition

Library of Congress Cataloging in Publication Control Number: 2023013666

Contents

Preface: The View from Science Fiction

The subtitle of this book—*A Science Fiction Writer Explores Atheism, Agnosticism, and the Idea of God*—might seem at first sight like a colossal non sequitur, on the order of "a plumber's guide to Broadway choreography" or "brain surgery for real estate agents." And I'm aware that for some readers the words *science fiction* will immediately translate to *non-serious* (or something worse). But as I hope to show, the connection between the science fiction genre and the debate about the existence of God is deeper, older, more interesting, and more thoughtful than you might expect. Science fiction is a literature that inevitably raises questions about the past, the future, and what it means to be human, and the answers it offers often contrast or conflict with conventional religious ideas about human origins and human destiny. That conflict can shed light in both directions. There is, in other words, a "view from science fiction" worth taking, and that's the view I'll be taking in this book.

I began writing *Owning the Unknown* with two purposes in mind. One was to mount a defense of what I call intuitive atheism: the atheism of those who haven't studied the philosophical and theological arguments for and against theism but who "just don't believe in God." That has probably always been the commonest kind of atheism, and there is some evidence that it's an increasingly popular one. According to a 2019 Pew Research Center poll, while the number of Americans who explicitly identify as atheists or agnostics has grown only modestly since 2009, the category of those who describe their religion as "nothing in particular" saw a significant increase. Similarly, some prominent Christians have worried that a greater threat to their faith than traditional atheism is "apatheism," a sense that questions about the existence of god are largely irrelevant or ultimately unanswerable. A 2021 editorial in the *National Catholic Register* frets about what the author David Mills calls "yeah, whatever" atheism: "There's no God to be found, but you can think about him if you want. There's no meaning to your life that you can find, but if you feel like it, you can ponder this too . . . it's relaxed atheism, a casual unconcerned atheism, even genial atheism, but it's still atheism." Arguing with this kind of atheism, according to Mills, is "like boxing with a big foam pillow or a giant marshmallow. Every time you land a punch it dimples a little, but then in a few seconds the dimple pops out."[1] *Owning the Unknown* aims to defend the rationality of these "genial atheisms."

Owning the Unknown isn't a work of philosophy, except in the broadest sense that any discussion of atheism or agnosticism borders on philosophy. It doesn't attempt to refute or endorse any of the formal philosophical arguments for or against the existence of God, though it does, at least briefly, describe some of those arguments and ask what they're meant to accomplish. With a couple of simple exceptions, the language of academic philosophy isn't the language I use in this book. *Owning the Unknown* makes a different and more intimate argument: that intuitive atheism is rooted in a reasonable assessment of personal knowledge, and that a rational entailment of that assessment is not just a vague agnosticism but a robust, defensible atheism.

The second purpose of this book is to approach its subject in the context of my experience as a professional writer working in a genre with deep roots in Enlightenment rationalism and a penchant for freewheeling speculation.

When I first began reading science fiction, the genre was little more than a quirky, low-rent appendage to the paperback publishing industry; and when I first began to call myself an atheist, atheism was still a fringe philosophy largely consigned to the beatnik-haunted back streets of American culture. By the time I began to acquire some professional credentials—my first novel was published in 1986—the cultural status of both atheism and science fiction was clearly changing. Science fiction had begun to move from the margins to a central place in the entertainment industry, and atheism was, if not entirely respectable, at least less likely to be taken as *prima facie* evidence of moral depravity. By the end of the first decade of the twenty-first century, I had won some major awards, my work was in print in more than a dozen languages, and science fiction was an inescapable fixture at the Cineplex, on the small screen, and in the publishing industry. Atheism, meanwhile, had been boosted into prominence by writers like Richard Dawkins and Christopher Hitchens, to the point where it became commonplace to speak about "the new atheism." These parallel trajectories, I would suggest, are not entirely coincidental.

I've spent most of my life as an "out" atheist, and occasionally in the past I've thought about writing a systematic defense of intuitive atheism—if not a book, then an essay, a blog post, a Twitter thread, *something*. And, just as often, I've considered writing about the way science fiction has tracked the cultural upheavals that followed from the industrial revolution and the technological and scientific churn of the twentieth century (and I have published a couple of brief essays that touch on that subject). But nothing substantial came of either project until I realized they were essentially the *same* project. The impulse that steered my career as a writer is the same impulse that motivated my atheism, and the

boundary where fiction and science meet philosophy and speculation is a place where interesting sparks have been struck and where
a brighter light might be shed.

My hope is that self-identified atheists and agnostics will discover in this book a different way of thinking about their atheism
and agnosticism, that those familiar with science fiction will enjoy
looking at the genre from a new angle, and that those unacquaint-
ed with science fiction will find it to be it an entertaining and
surprisingly useful lens through which to examine the questions
posed by our shared religious traditions. Because the content of
this book is partially autobiographical, I'll be talking primarily
about Christianity and Christian theism, but the major points are
applicable to other faiths in ways that should be readily apparent.
Committed Christians will no doubt find much to disagree with,
but I've tried to frame the discussion in a way that doesn't casually
dismiss or deride their point of view. And for those curious about
what the intersection of atheism, science, and literature looks like
in practice, I have included in an appendix two of my own short
stories that reflect, in one way or another, the concerns of this
book.

* * *

The ideas expressed in *Owning the Unknown* have evolved over
many years, and it would be impossible to thank everyone who
has contributed to it. Countless half-forgotten conversations have
played into the writing of this book—with friends over coffee in
late-night restaurants, with colleagues at conventions and on book
tours, and with Christian and atheist bloggers in the murky depths
of online comment threads. If you think you might be among that
number, you probably are, and I thank you. And, as always, I have
to express my gratitude to my wife, whose reserves of patience and
tolerance are apparently bottomless: thanks yet again, Sharry.

OWNING THE UNKNOWN

1

Does God Exist?
Maybe That's the Wrong Question

I was a week away from my thirteenth birthday when I first attended a church function voluntarily and without the company of my parents. It was a Wednesday night in December, the weather in the Toronto suburb where we lived was cold and getting colder, and I walked the three blocks from our house to the local Baptist church at a brisk pace, pausing only once or twice to kick at the crusts of ice that had begun to congeal on curbside puddles.

I wasn't ordinarily enthusiastic about church or anything connected with it. I managed to sit through Sunday services without complaining—usually—but I had resisted Sunday school so often and so vocally that my parents finally let me skip it altogether. But this occasion was different. What had lured me out into the chilly night was the promise of a display of ultraviolet fluorescence.

Two Sundays ago I had spotted an announcement in the mimeographed bulletin tucked into the pews next to the Bibles and the hymn books. The subject was something about gospel stories for children and teens, but it was the line promising "a glow-in-the-dark black light presentation" that caused my own eyes to light up. I was a precocious reader, already fascinated by anything related to science, and lately I had been reading about the physics of light, possibly in one of Isaac Asimov's science guides for general readers. And although there was much I didn't understand, I had successfully grasped the concept of ultraviolet light—that is, light of a frequency beyond the visible spectrum, a kind of light human eyes can't see. And I knew UV light would cause certain dyes to fluoresce in glowing, gaudy colors. This was the mid-1960s, a few years before black-light Jimi Hendrix posters became a fixture in the bedrooms of suburban teenagers, and I was determined to see the phenomenon for myself, even if it came at the price of a sermon.

I bounded up the church stairs, left my winter jacket on a peg in the cloak room, and followed a trail of handmade signs to a meeting room off the main chapel where folding chairs had been set up in front of an easel. A pair of amiable adults—maybe the resident Sunday school teachers; I didn't recognize them—glanced at the wall clock and eventually introduced themselves to the gathered multitude, about a dozen adolescents including myself. Most of the attendees were around my own age, and only a few seemed enthusiastic about what was to come. But we dutifully took our seats when we were asked to.

The doors were closed. The presentation began. Disappointment immediately set in. Propped on the easel was a flannel board. Flannel boards, also called flannelgraphs, were visual aids then (and apparently still) popular with evangelical Sunday schools. The board was covered with a swatch of fuzzy cloth to which fabric cutouts of Bible characters could be affixed for the purpose of illustrating a story. Tonight's story, unsurprisingly, was the Nativity. For several interminable minutes the two youth evangelists escorted a slightly threadbare Joseph and Mary from one palm-tree-and-donkey mise-en-scène to the next. No black light. I was on the verge of raising an objection—false advertising!—until we reached the manger, the star, the wise men from the east. That was when a girl at the back of the room was delegated to turn off the overhead lights.

One of the teachers switched on a UV source mounted over the easel, and the Star of Bethlehem promptly lit up like a plum-colored supernova. So did the manger, the holy family, the magi, their gifts; so did various loose threads, dust specks, and stitched hems on our shirts and shoes. The woman at the flannelgraph wore a hairband that radiated a blue glow like an icy halo.

I knew how this worked. Energetic but invisible UV photons struck chemical compounds in the dyed fabric like incoming ordnance, causing the atoms to kick out new photons at a lower, visible energy level. The result was this wonderfully ghostly coral-reef radiance. The Nativity story itself was infinitely less interesting, familiar not just from church but from school pageants and the Christmas specials that aired on television every year around this time. I was already a science fiction reader, though not a particularly sophisticated one, and I understood the Nativity in science-fictional terms: a cosmic being makes contact with Earth by sending an emissary disguised as a human child. It was a neat enough idea. It reminded me of a John Wyndham paperback I had recently read, *Village of the Damned*, in which aliens plant their hybrid offspring in the wombs of unsuspecting women in a small English town—though this version would have to be called *Village of the Blessed*. The premise was good, I thought, although the Gospel narrative that followed from it was more than a little confusing. But I wasn't here for the storytelling. I was here to see the world made incandescent by invisible radiation.

And so it was, though it ended all too soon. The overhead lights were switched on. The flannelgraph morphed back into a low-rent Sunday-school prop. The woman with the radiant hairband took a seat, and the man who had helped her narrate the story smiled and asked whether we had any questions.

I raised my hand. He nodded at me.

I stood up. "Bees," I said, collecting my thoughts.

"Bees?"

"Did you know they can see ultraviolet light? Bees, I mean. They have eyes that can see ultraviolet light. It helps them find flowers."

Someone giggled. The teacher thanked me for that interesting information and looked pointedly for another raised hand. I sat back down, blushing. All this was followed soon enough by an invitation to commit our lives to Christ.

Altar calls inevitably made me uncomfortable, whether in church or at the climax of the Billy Graham rallies my parents watched on TV. I didn't understand them. The smiling adult standing at the flannel board seemed well-intentioned, but it was as if he wanted me to sign a contract I hadn't read or buy a product I wasn't sure I wanted. So I slumped in my chair, hoping not to be noticed, and when that tactic failed I pled the necessity of a bathroom call, rescued my jacket from the cloakroom, and escaped into the December night.

Snow had started to fall. Fat, perfect snowflakes danced to gusts of wind, made gauzy circles around streetlights, blurred the lenses of my glasses. The bees had all gone wherever bees go in winter, but I wondered what a bee might see on a night like this. What I had said was true: bees and many other insects are sensitive to ultraviolet light, and flowers that have evolved to attract pollinating insects often display patterns invisible to human eyes. (I imagined petals lit up in luminous grids, like cities seen at night from an airplane.) Did crystals of snow, too, scatter light in colors beyond purple? Was this blanket of monochromatic whiteness, for some other creature, a glittering rainbow?

I was happy enough with the evening, though it taught me I shouldn't entirely trust announcements in church bulletins. Whatever the intentions of the smiling and soft-spoken youth evangelists who conducted the session, I had been granted at least a quick glimpse of the world beyond its visible limits, a token of a realm not ordinarily available to human senses. (It didn't occur to me then that the evangelists might have described their faith the same way.)

But the event left other questions in my mind, more troubling ones. Why did so many people want me to hold a certain opinion about God, and to declare that opinion publicly? Why did Bible stories, presented as fact, feature so many of the hallmarks of fantasy—miracles, apparitions both demonic and angelic, covenants negotiated with cosmic powers? What exactly was I being asked to believe, and why did it *matter*? I didn't mind singing along with the hymns on Sunday—or at least mouthing the words and pretending—but if someone were to ask the question directly, how would I answer it? *Did* I believe in God? Or was I that unmentionable thing, an atheist?

* * *

No one knows when the existence of God was first asserted or denied, but the question has probably been asked about some conception of a divine being for as long as human beings have had the capacity to ask it. Most if not all of our familiar religious faiths began as rebellions against or amendments to earlier orthodoxies and priesthoods, which means that atheism—in the broadest sense of the rejection of some *particular* conception of a divine being—is inseparable from the history of religion and arguably just as venerable.

The pharaoh Amenhotep IV came to power in Egypt around the year 1351 BC, at a time when Egypt's Eighteenth Dynasty was the ancient Near East's dominant cultural and military power. The kingdom he inherited was blessed, or burdened, with a wildly diverse system of polytheistic beliefs. Egyptians of the day worshipped a confusing pantheon of deities—Isis, Anubis, Osiris, among many others—whose priesthoods competed for the patronage of the powerful and the wealthy. Amenhotep's reign began conventionally enough, but after five years on the throne, he made the decision to consolidate power in a wholly radical way: by establishing a new religion with himself as its divine head. He changed his pharaonic name to Akhenaten, elevated the relatively obscure sun god Aten to a central place in his cosmology, ordered shrines to Aten built in various Egyptian cities, and began construction of an entirely new capital, Akhetaten, at an uninhabited spot on the Nile halfway between Cairo and Luxor—today a dusty archeological site called Amarna, where the limestone and mud-brick ruins of the ancient city bake in summer heat that regularly approaches 40 degrees Celsius. And in the ninth year of his reign, at the apex of his power, Akhenaten declared Aten to be not just the greatest of the gods, but the *only* god. He further declared that he himself was Aten's son and that Egyptians would henceforth worship Aten by way of worshipping Akhenaten.

"The history of ancient Egypt," the historian Anne Applebaum has written, "looks, from a great distance in time, like a monotonous story of interchangeable pharaohs. But on closer examination, it includes periods of cultural lightness and eras of despotic gloom."[1] A statue preserved in the Egyptian Museum of Cairo makes the youthful Akhenaten appear benign, even amiable—but that's what court artists are hired for. In fact, his reign was gloomily despotic by almost any definition. At Akhenaten's command, according to historian Jonathan Kirsch, "the shrines and temples of rival deities were closed, the rituals of worship were suppressed, the statues that symbolized the other deities were shattered, and their names and images were literally chiseled off the stone monuments of ancient Egypt. The high priest of Amon, whose services were no longer needed, was put to work in a stone quarry like a common slave."[2]

Akhenaten, we might say, had placed himself in a relation of atheism to these prior gods. If he didn't entirely deny their existence, he at least claimed that the old gods had grown toothless and ineffectual; their time had come and gone. But in the end, despite all the destruction he wreaked, Akhenaten's forcible reformation failed. After his death the old gods made a hasty comeback. Akhenaten's first major successor, the pharaoh Tutankhamun—"King Tut," whose nearly intact tomb was famously unearthed by the British archeologist Howard Carter in 1922—moved the royal court back to Thebes and chose for himself a name that honored Amun, the most popular of the gods whose worship Akhenaten had targeted for extinction. The pharaohs who followed Tutankhamun continued his restoration, and Seti I, the first pharaoh of the Nineteenth Dynasty, ordered the name of Amun chiseled back onto the monuments from which it had been effaced. Percy Bysshe Shelley's 1818 poem "Ozymandias" was inspired by a different pharaoh (Ramesses II), but the poet could as easily have been describing Akhenaten and the sun-wracked ruins of modern Amarna when he wrote,

Nothing beside remains. Round the decay
Of that colossal wreck, boundless and bare
The lone and level sands stretch far away.

There are many morals to this story. The most obvious is that human history is littered with the debris of discarded gods, a truth more than one atheist has used to belabor an opponent. The nineteenth-century American writer and political figure Robert G. Ingersoll—a Civil War veteran, Republican kingmaker, and self-declared agnostic, famous for his scandalous but popular lectures on the follies of religion—made that argument at length in an essay called "The Gods." "Each nation has created a god," Ingersoll declared, "and the god has always resembled his creators. He hated and loved what they hated and loved, and he was invariably on the side of those in power. Each god was intensely patriotic, and detested all nations but his own. . . . All these gods have insisted upon having a vast number of priests, and the priests have always insisted upon being supported by the people, and the principal business of these priests has been to boast about their god, and to insist that he could easily vanquish all the other gods put together."[3] This is true, and funny—the whole lecture is available online and well worth reading—but is it helpful?

Christians will object that gods like Aten and Amun are nothing like the God of Christianity, and in an important sense they're right, but let's see if we can tease another truth out of the story, one that won't immediately provoke an argument. One thing we notice is that the gods, even insurgent gods like Akhenaten's, don't arise *de novo*. Gods are born of other gods, or are defined in relation to them. Aten was a minor sun deity for centuries—the name appears in the Abusir Papyri, dated to around the twenty-fourth century BC—before Akhenaten promoted him to the center of the universe, and the gods Aten temporarily displaced have long histories of their own, their own eras of relative favor and disfavor. What may seem at first glance like religious innovations are seldom actually new. In the Book of Genesis we find traces of an earlier Hebrew polytheism; the Christian gospels place Jesus squarely in the context of Judaic law and prophecy; Islam acknowledges Moses and Jesus as prophets; the Book of Mormon mimics the prose of the King James Bible, and so *ad seriatim*. Archeological digs in Shaanxi Province in China have found tombs dated to circa 4500–3750 BC in which the dead were buried along with earthly goods, suggesting a belief in an afterlife; during the Shang Dynasty (1600–1046 BC), there was a flourishing pantheon of major and minor deities. In Europe and the Middle East we find evidence of religious practices as old as the Middle Paleolithic period, arguably including Neanderthal sites. There is no historical moment to which we can point and say, "Here begins religion." Religion has existed, in other words, for as long as modern humans have walked the earth, and possibly longer. And the equally venerable tradition of punishing religious dissent, whether or not we call that dissent "heresy," suggests that religion plays an important role in the way human communities define themselves and police their cultural and political boundaries.

In other words, the ubiquity and persistence of religion has shaped the way we think and talk about it. This is as true in the twenty-first century as it was in Akhenaten's day. In the contemporary West our way of talking about God has been shaped by a complex set of influences, from pagan philosophy to the Catholic Magisterium, from Plato to Thomas Aquinas to David Hume, from the Renaissance to the Reformation to the Age of Enlightenment. This is the theater in which the dialogue between theism and atheism customarily takes place, this is the language it speaks, and this is where we stand when we add our voices to that debate.

Philosophers in the Western tradition have insisted that words must be carefully defined, and from that imperative we arrive at the most common definition of God in Christian theism. God is the source of all things, a creator being who is maximally good (omnibenevolent), maximally powerful (omnipotent), maximally knowing (omniscient), and everywhere at once (omnipresent). Philosophers have often sought to pin down the question of what we mean by "exists" in this context. Does God exist in the way material objects exist, in the way ideas exist, or in some other way? We have to tread carefully here, for the claim made by the most sophisticated advocates for theism is not simply *God exists* but something more like:

> *God (for certain definitions of "God")*
> *exists (for certain definitions of "exists").*

Christian theology and Western philosophy have grown in tandem, in other words, and when we talk about God we do so from within an intellectual framework both traditions have helped to construct. Is it possible to step outside of that conceptual framework, and can we learn anything of value by doing so?

Christians often insist that atheism is obliged to address the best arguments for theism in order to reject it, and there's certainly some merit to that argument. But it can't be *entirely* true, even from the Christian perspective. If atheists need a solid understanding of Aquinas or Anselm before they can reasonably dismiss the existence of God then, logically, Christians need the same solid understanding before they can reasonably assert it. But that's not what happens in practice. Jesus, in the Book of Matthew, instructs his followers to "go and make disciples of all nations, baptizing them in the name of the Father and of the Son and of the Holy Spirit," not to ensure that potential converts are well-versed in the Platonic theory of essences before they consider devoting their lives to Christ.

And how practical is it for anyone, theist or atheist, to master in detail centuries of theological and philosophical debate? The vast majority of us necessarily stand outside of that discourse. At best, we might have a couple of university-level survey courses behind us. And yet, Christians insist, we're obliged to choose—does God exist or not?—and the choice we make, they say, will have profound consequences, if not in this life then in the next.

Moreover—this is an important point—we can't turn to philosophy to definitively answer the question of God's existence. Western philosophy raises the question, it defines the question, it explores the question, it speculates systematically about potential answers, it offers arguments and counterarguments, and all this is good and useful and interesting, but it doesn't yield a final answer or a reliable common consensus. In his textbook *Metaphysics*, the Christian philosopher Peter van Inwagen acknowledges that metaphysical philosophy doesn't produce "results" the way, for instance, the sciences produce a body of reliable knowledge:

> In the end we must confess that we have no idea why there is no established body of metaphysical results. It cannot be denied that this is a fact, however, and the beginning student of metaphysics should keep this fact and its implications in mind. One of its implications is that neither the author of this book nor your instructor (if you are reading this book because it is

an assigned text) is in a position in relation to you that is like the position of the author of your text (or your instructor) in geology or tax law or music theory. All these people will be the masters of a certain body of knowledge, and, on many matters, if you disagree with them you will simply be wrong. In metaphysics, however, you are perfectly free to disagree with anything the acknowledged experts say—other than their assertions about what philosophers have said in the past or are saying at present.[4]

This is worth remembering. The existence of the Christian God is an inherently metaphysical question and an intrinsically unsettled one. If you delve into the philosophy of metaphysics in search of a single reliable answer to the question of God's existence, you won't find one. What you will find is a myriad of answers, a myriad of rebuttals to those answers, and a debate that has endured for centuries without reaching a demonstrably reliable conclusion. (Which is not to disparage philosophy in general or metaphysics in particular. For these disciplines, in many ways, the debate *is* the point.)

So where does that leave us, as embodied human beings, situated as we are at a particular point in time and space and human history, each of us with a unique range of experiences and education, as we grapple with questions about God?

* * *

As I hurried down the church steps that December evening, snowflakes settling like silt through a sea of winter air, I didn't know that I had embarked on a lifetime of exploring these ideas—tangentially, as a writer of science fiction, and sometimes directly, as a self-defined atheist with a layman's interest in philosophy and religion.

Ancient Egypt was a mystery to me, but I would have been at least dimly aware that Osiris and Anubis were on the list of gods no longer worshipped and that their reigns had been temporary and pyrrhic. The mid-century American science fiction I was beginning to read had much to say about the rise and fall of civilizations. Isaac Asimov in his Foundation trilogy reimagined Edward Gibbon's history of the Roman Empire on a galactic stage; Walter M. Miller Jr., in his landmark novel *A Canticle for Leibowitz*, envisioned a new Dark Age following a global nuclear war and speculated about the role the Church might play in preserving endangered knowledge. The lesson I took from these and other stories was that, while religion might persist, its particular expression was as mutable and as ephemeral as any other human cultural act. In a thousand or two thousand years there might not be a Christianity, or there might be a Christianity so altered by the passage of time as to be unrecognizable from where we currently stand. Soon enough I began to call myself an atheist, or at least an agnostic, since those labels appeared to match most closely the answers toward which I was groping. It was only as an adult that I began to wonder whether the question itself might be part of the problem.

But if "does God exist?" has no single reliable answer, is there a better question we can ask?

2

Fiat Lux: What We Can Learn from Classical Arguments for the Existence of God

Most of us have heard of the Big Bang, if only through countless references in popular culture, including the long-running American television sitcom of the same name. That might be because, stripped of the painstaking observation and calculation that went into its formulation, the idea of the Big Bang is both surprising and fairly easy to grasp. The universe is expanding, which means it was once much smaller—small enough that everything around us, from Earth to the farthest star, was once concentrated in a single inconceivably dense and unimaginably hot point. ("Our whole universe was in a hot, dense state," as the sitcom theme song has it.) The Big Bang is the expansion of this point—not a point *in* space and time, but a point *of* space and time—out of which matter as we know it precipitated like snow from a cloud of primordial plasma, eventually enabling the formation of stars like our sun and planets like the one we call home.

The originator of this idea was a Catholic priest, Fr. Georges

Lemaître, a mathematician, astronomer, and former Belgian army artillery officer who for years was a professor of physics at the Catholic University of Louvain. Lemaître called his idea "the hypothesis of the primeval atom." "Big Bang," the name that stuck, was coined as a term of derision by the British astronomer Sir Fred Hoyle, who preferred to believe the universe existed in a steady state. Einstein, too, initially disliked Lemaître's idea, though he conceded that the math was impeccable. ("Your calculations are correct," he wrote to Lemaître, "but your physics is atrocious.")[1]

Hoyle and Einstein were wrong, however, and Einstein, at least, would go on to embrace the theory, though Hoyle remained a stubborn contrarian until his death in 2001. (Hoyle wrote some memorable science fiction along the way, of which his 1957 novel *The Black Cloud* is probably the best-known example.) In the 1950s Lemaître's work was also embraced—not entirely to Lemaître's liking—by Pope Pius XII. Pius XII, born Eugenio Pacelli, is today more often remembered for having signed a controversial treaty, the *Reichskonkordat*, between the Vatican and Nazi Germany when he served as the Vatican's Cardinal Secretary of State, but he was also "one of the unacknowledged super geeks in the history of the papacy," according to the science writer John Farrell, "a pope who preferred to eat his meals alone so he could immerse himself in science magazines and technology reviews."[2] Pius XII welcomed Lemaître's theory as a direct confirmation of divine creation. "Indeed," Pius wrote in 1951, "it would seem that present-day science, with one sweep back across the centuries, has succeeded in bearing witness to the august instant of the Fiat Lux, when, along with matter, there burst forth from nothing a sea of light and radiation, and the elements split and churned and formed into millions of galaxies."[3]

Lemaître was uneasy about the Pope's tacit endorsement of his conjecture, not least because there was, at the time, not yet decisive evidence for it—and the Pope was uneasy enough about Lemaître that he neglected to mention the astronomer's name even as he praised his hypothesis. Lemaître, who was both a Jesuit and a scientist, believed in a God who had set the universe in motion but allowed it to unfold according to natural law. His God was a *deus absconditus*, a hidden God, not inclined to put his finger on the cosmic scale. That idea offended conservative Catholics, who found it impossible to reconcile with the Biblical narrative of Adam and Eve. Only a year earlier, in the encyclical *Humani Generis*, Pius XII himself had affirmed that "the faithful in Christ cannot accept this view [of evolution], which holds...that Adam signifies some kind of multitude of first parents; for it is by no means apparent how such an opinion can be reconciled with what the sources of revealed truth and the acts of the magisterium of the Church teach about original sin."[4]

A few years later, Lemaître's uneasiness about his own theory was dispelled by the accumulation of supporting evidence from various sources. In 1964 two scientists at Bell Labs in New Jersey, Arno Penzias and Robert Wilson, were experimenting with a new kind of antenna meant to capture signals bounced off the Echo 1 satellites recently placed in low Earth orbit. Because the signals they were looking for were almost vanishingly faint, Penzias and Wilson needed to eliminate as much interference as possible from their receiving apparatus, including by cooling their receiver to -269 degrees Celsius in a bath of liquid helium. Despite those heroic efforts, one source of noise remained stubbornly persistent. It was a continuous hum that seemed to appear from every part of the sky at all times, regardless of the rotation of the earth or the direction of the antenna. After ruling out other possible sources of extraneous noise—at one point they evicted a family of pigeons that had nested in the antenna—Penzias and Wilson concluded that the signal was real and that it was coming from a source beyond our own galaxy.

What they had discovered was the cosmic background radiation, a predicted consequence of radiation from the early epoch of the Big Bang. That was solid evidence for Lemaître's conjecture, and by the late 1960s little doubt remained. The universe wasn't a stage on which stories were played out, like a cosmic flannel board. The universe *was* a story, with something like a beginning and something like an end.

Many Christian theologians have since endorsed the Big Bang scenario, not only because it jibes with at least a loose interpretation of the Genesis story but because it echoes a philosophical argument for the existence of God.

The tradition of formulating philosophical arguments designed to prove the existence of God is nearly as old as Christianity itself—in some ways, older. The aim of such arguments is to rationally deduce the existence of God from the observation of nature, without resorting to divine revelation. There are distinct families of such arguments, and a novice atheist dipping his toe in the waters of on-line debate will inevitably encounter all of them. Entire libraries of books have been devoted to defending or contesting them.

The argument to which the Big Bang theory is relevant is called the Cosmological Argument. There are many variations of it, but we'll look at one of the simpler ones. Our purpose here is not to dispute the argument but to take it as a representative sample of Christian philosophical argumentation and to reverse-engineer it—to ask where it came from, how it works, what its functioning parts are, and whether it gets us any closer to answering the question of God's existence.

* * *

One version of the argument is sometimes called the Kalam Cosmological Argument. "Kalam" is from *'ilm al-kalam*, an Arabic term for Islamic theology. The modern Christian philosopher William Lane Craig, who gave his formulation of the argument that name, attributes the earliest version of it to Al-Ghazali, an influential eleventh-century Sunni Muslim philosopher and mystic. Al-Ghazali produced, among other works, a book with the appealing title *The Incoherence of the Philosophers* (to which the Muslim scholar Ibn Rushid, known as Averroes, wrote a rebuttal called *The Incoherence of the Incoherence* . . . and so it goes).

The roots of the argument are even older. The Thomistic version of the Cosmological Argument (after the thirteenth-century Christian scholar Thomas Aquinas) depends on ideas about causality borrowed from the pre-Christian philosopher Aristotle, for instance. We can see in this family of arguments a kind of shadow history of Western philosophy. Ideas born in classical Hellenic philosophy, exiled by the official Christianity of the late Roman world, traveled east and took root during Islam's medieval Golden Age; these same ideas found new expression in the West through the work of early Christian philosophers such as Aquinas (whose writing included extensive commentaries on Aristotle), influenced the cultural and social changes that comprised the European Renaissance, and in turn influenced the rise of Enlightenment humanism and modern academic philosophy. If the Cosmological Argument owned a passport, it would be stamped by principalities from the Arabian Peninsula to the shores of the North Sea. Listen closely to it and you might hear water splashing in the fountains of Al-Andalus, a lateen sail rippling as it catches the breeze from Tyre to Alexandria, or footsteps ticking on the foggy streets of sixteenth-century Amsterdam.

There are too many variations of the argument to treat individually, and, again, we aren't trying to refute it. If you want to engage it at that level, there are countless books, articles, blog posts, and websites where that discussion happens on a daily basis, at every level of discourse from formal philosophy to YouTube debates to grammatically challenged meme wars. For our purposes, we'll look at the version presented and defended by the contemporary Christian writer William Lane Craig, to see if we can learn anything that might apply more generally.

Here is the heart of the argument as Craig presents it:

1. Everything that begins to exist has a cause of its existence.

2. The universe began to exist.

3. Therefore, the universe has a cause of its existence.

4. Since no scientific explanation (in terms of physical laws) can provide a causal account of the origin (very beginning) of the universe, the cause must be personal (explanation is given in terms of a personal agent).[5]

The first thing we might notice is that this takes the form of a syllogism, a deductive argument in which the stated premises necessitate the conclusion. A simpler example:

1. The only person at this party wearing a white tie and a fedora is named Bob.

2. This dude is wearing a white tie and a fedora.

3. This dude must be Bob.

That's a logically valid syllogism. Whether it's true depends on whether the premises are sound. Logically valid syllogisms can be constructed from unsound premises:

1. All cats are made of marzipan.

2. Anything made of marzipan comes from Mars.

3. All cats are from Mars.

In which case the conclusion, while it follows logically from the premises—and while it may have a certain intuitive appeal for cat owners—is also probably unsound.

In Craig's version of the Cosmological Argument you might think it's the fourth proposition that runs into trouble, and you wouldn't be alone in that suspicion—but let's set that aside and look instead at the first three (much simpler) premises.

* * *

Premise 1: *Everything that begins to exist has a cause of its existence.*

As we said, the Cosmological Argument is an example of what is sometimes called natural theology: an argument that aims to deduce the existence of God from reason and observation, as opposed to divine revelation, mystical experience, or the interpretation of scripture. Once again, we find the roots of this approach in the pre-Christian world. "Now as for all the heaven," Plato wrote in *Timaeus*, "(or cosmos, or whatever else it may be most receptive to being called ...) the first thing about it one must investigate is ... whether it always was, having no beginning of a coming to be, or whether it has come to be, having begun from some beginning."

For Craig's formulation to succeed as natural theology it needs to move from observational truths to a metaphysical conclusion—from "everything that begins to exist has a cause" to the existence of a transcendental, all-creating God. In other words, it aims to build a ladder from what we *observe* to be the case to what *must* be the case for all reality at all times and all places. "The point of the argument," Craig says, "is to demonstrate the existence of a first cause which transcends and creates *the entire realm of finite reality*" [emphasis mine].[6]

So the first premise presents itself as an observable truth. And at first glance, that's exactly what it seems to be. The proposition that "everything that begins to exist has a cause of its existence" accords with our everyday experience. If I want chili for dinner, I have to cook up a batch—or open a can, or order from a restaurant; in any case, a bowl of chili isn't going to appear spontaneously on the dinner table, more's the pity. Something has to *cause* it to be there. And that seems to be true of everything from bluebirds to black holes. So is Premise 1 sound?

Maybe. Many arguments have been made to buttress it, drawing from mathematics (the alleged impossibility of actual infinities or an infinite causal series), for instance, or from simple intuition ("the metaphysical intuition that something cannot come out of nothing," as Craig describes it). And, of course, all these arguments for the soundness of the premise have been countered by arguments *against* the soundness of the premise. And so it goes.

But, again, maybe that's the wrong question. Let's ask a more personal one, a question we can each answer for ourselves: *Do I know whether Premise 1 is sound?*

Look at it more closely. Premise 1 is a proposition about "everything that begins to exist." Am I in a position to make confident assertions about "everything that begins to exist"? That's a tall order, since "everything" includes . . . well, *everything*. Not just "everything in my experience" or "everything in my immediate vicinity." *Everything*. "All the heaven," as Plato says, "or cosmos, or whatever else it may be most receptive to being called." The entire realm of finite reality. After all, even one exception defeats the proposition. For Premise 1 to be true, it must be absolutely and universally true.

But my personal knowledge of "the entire realm of finite reality" is, to say the least, partial. My knowledge has conspicuous gaps and self-evident limitations. The farther it extends from my immediate environment, the more tentative and second-hand my knowledge becomes. I know the keyboard on which I'm typing these words didn't spring into being *de novo*; I know it had a cause, as causes are conventionally understood. But there are open scientific questions about causality at the subatomic level, for instance. I don't pretend to entirely or, in most cases, even partially *understand* these controversies, but I know that quantum causality is controversial among those who do understand it, in ways that challenge our everyday experience of cause and effect.

Moreover, the world I can observe, even in principle, is only a fractional subset of "the entire realm of finite reality." My knowledge becomes partial and tentative long before it reaches the primordial past, the most plausibly foreseeable distant future, the tiniest realms of matter and energy, or whatever might exist of the cosmos beyond its perceptible limits.

* * *

Remember that the goal of the Cosmological Argument is to reason from observable truths to a *metaphysical* truth. Metaphysics can be a difficult discipline to pin down, so let's hit pause for a moment and stipulate a definition for the purposes of this book. Quoting the Merriam-Webster dictionary, metaphysics is "a division of philosophy that is concerned with the fundamental nature of reality and being." The Collins dictionary offers "the philosophical study of the nature of reality," and other brief definitions follow along the same lines. The subject is vastly more nuanced than that, of course, but what most of these definitions have in common is the idea that metaphysics is reasoning about reality at its most complete, most irreducible, most all-inclusive level. When we reason about observable phenomena (rocks, animals, stars, atoms), we're usually doing science or something like it. When we reason about the nature of existence itself, we're doing metaphysics. There are other definitions, but for the purposes of this book, I'll consistently use the word in this *particular* sense:

Metaphysics is reasoning about the nature of reality
at all times and all places.

Propositions that are limited to the observable universe may be scientific propositions, or historical propositions, or may fall into similar categories, but they are not metaphysical propositions.

Which points up an important ambiguity in the Cosmological Argument. Recall that the aim of the argument is to deduce the existence of "a first cause which transcends and creates the entire realm of finite reality"—in other words, to leverage metaphysical knowledge from mutually agreed-upon observable truths.

Is Premise 1 a mutually agreed-upon observable truth?

Examined closely, no, it isn't. If Premise 1 were merely a claim about our observable fraction of reality, it wouldn't be entitled to the word "everything." Revise it to "*Some* things that begin to exist have a cause" or "*Many* things that begin to exist have a cause," or even "*Most* things that begin to exist have a cause," and the argument collapses. Premise 1 succeeds for Craig's purposes only if it fully and accurately describes *all* of reality, no matter how remote in time or space and no matter how ontologically distant from us. Premise 1 is *itself* a metaphysical claim.

Which means that, from its first premise, the Kalam Cosmological Argument deploys a metaphysical assertion to leverage a metaphysical conclusion. That's a pattern we can look for, and will often find, in other common arguments for the existence of God.

And from a purely personal standpoint, to answer my own question—no, I don't know whether the first premise of Craig's syllogism is sound. In other words, I'm *agnostic* about that proposition.

* * *

Let's pause a second time to define "agnostic" and "gnostic" for the purposes of this book.

"Agnosticism" is commonly used to describe the belief that the existence of God is either unknown or unknowable. I want to set aside that usage and deploy the word in a more general sense. "Agnostic" derives from the Greek ágnōstos, which might be translated as "without knowledge," and that's the sense in which I intend to use it. (Another word describing lack of knowledge is "ignorance," but that has pejorative connotations best avoided.) Throughout this book I'll be using "agnostic" to characterize a simple lack of knowledge, whether or not in the context of theological debate. I might say, for instance, that I am personally *agnostic* about the history of Japanese pottery, without implying that the history of

Japanese pottery is either unknown or unknowable.

Similarly, in the case of the Kalam Cosmological Argument, I am *agnostic* about the soundness of Premise 1. I simply don't know whether it's true or false. More than that: It would be both irrational and *dishonest* for me, situated as I am, and with the knowledge I currently possess, to concede that Premise 1 is true.

* * *

Premise 2: *The universe began to exist.*

See yonder, lo, the Galaxyë
Which men clepeth the Milky Wey,

wrote Geoffrey Chaucer in his poem *The House of Fame*, circa 1380, in what etymologists believe is the first recorded use of the term "Milky Way." The word "galaxy" has a more complicated history, but it was originally just a synonym for the horizon-spanning arch of pearlescent light once familiar to anyone with a view of the clear night sky. Today, thanks to light pollution, a modern city-dweller might grow up and grow old without ever catching sight of the Milky Way in all its glory. But anyone who has camped in a national park, for instance, will have had a chance to see our native galaxy just as vividly as Plato or Aristotle might have seen it on a moonless Athenian night.

To call it our *native* galaxy is to invoke very recent astronomical knowledge. The insightful Greek philosopher Democritus, better known for his theory that matter was made up of tiny indivisible components, *atomos* (which is just the Greek word for "indivisible"), argued that the Milky Way might be composed of distant stars. But that was far from a universally-held opinion. Aristotle believed the Milky Way marked the boundary between the celestial and terrestrial spheres, in a cosmological model that hasn't fared well over the last two thousand years. Galileo, in his *Sidereus*

Nuncius (1610), revealed that through the lens of his telescope at least parts of the Milky Way did indeed resolve into individual stars, helping to drive a final stake into whatever remained of Aristotle's model. Still unanswered, however, was the relationship of the Milky Way to our own sun and to the "nebulae"—fuzzy luminous objects visible in more modern telescopes.

The astronomer William Herschell was fascinated by these objects and identified over 5,000 nebulae, many with distinct disc-like or spiral shapes. And he wasn't alone in his fascination. By the time Herschell's son John published his catalogue of nebulae in 1864 the objects had already been the subject of much speculation, some of it from philosophers as august as Immanuel Kant, who argued that the Milky Way was a kind of "island universe" of which our solar system was a part, and that the nebulae might be other island universes, more distant in space. It was a prescient idea, but at the time there was no way to confirm or disprove it. That changed in the early twentieth century, when the astronomer Edwin Hubble began to make observations with the 100-inch Hooker telescope in California—at the time of its completion the largest telescope in the world.

The Hooker telescope was installed at the Mount Wilson Observatory in the San Gabriel Mountains near Pasadena in the year 1917. The English poet Alfred Noyes, present for its ceremonial inauguration, recorded the moment in his poem cycle *Watchers of the Sky*. The observatory loomed "like some great cathedral dome" against the night sky, Noyes wrote, revealing

> all those cloudless throngs of glittering stars
> And all those glimmerings where the abyss of space
> Is powdered with a milky dust, each grain
> A burning sun . . .

In 1922, using results from the Hooker Telescope, Edwin Hubble was finally able to resolve the long-standing question. The Milky Way was, yes, a galaxy (an "island universe"), in which our sun was one of millions bound together by the force of gravity; and the nebulae were, as Kant had speculated, other such "island universes," vastly farther away.

Hubble was also instrumental in the discovery that these island universes were moving away from one another, a key piece of evidence for George Lemaître's conjecture about the Primordial Atom. We can begin to see why Pius XII and later generations of Christian apologists were so elated by that discovery. Here, apparently, was scientific confirmation of the idea put forward by Christian philosophers from Thomas Aquinas to modern times, that the universe had a beginning . . . and perhaps an ultimate cause.

But Hubble's and Lemaître's discoveries raise another question about the Cosmological Argument: What do we mean when we use the word "universe"? Are we talking about "the entire realm of finite reality," or do we mean the vast array of stars and galaxies our telescopes have revealed in increasing depth and detail?

These are not the same things, and the word "universe" in the second premise of Craig's argument harbors an important ambiguity. As before, we have to ask ourselves whether the second premise is a scientific or a metaphysical assertion.

Kant's intuition that our galaxy might not be the only "island universe" has a parallel in modern scientific cosmology. We know that all we can possibly see from where we stand is not the sum of all that exists. To take just one example, what we can observe even in principle is limited by what physicists call the cosmological horizon—the maximum distance light could have traveled to reach an observer during the age of the universe. According to general relativity, information can't travel faster than the speed of light. That means that anything beyond the cosmological horizon is effectively and permanently hidden from us (though we may be able to draw inferences about it from what we *do* observe).

Moreover, extrapolating backward in time to the Big Bang doesn't bring us to a distinct act of creation—a Fiat Lux—so much as to a mire of confusion. Physicists won't fully understand what happened in the first picosecond of the Big Bang until they learn how to reconcile general relativity (which describes gravity, space and time) with quantum physics (which describes events on the very smallest scales, including the scale into which the universe was compressed at the very beginning of its expansion). Solving that mystery is one of the great outstanding projects of modern science.

The fog of uncertainty around these issues has left room for speculation about the possible existence of other universes, some perhaps quite different from the one in which we live. Any hypothesis featuring more than one physical universe is a "multiverse" theory, and the physicist Brian Greene has helpfully provided a bestiary of no less than nine types of plausible multiverse, including the possibility that our observable universe shares its existence with others in a higher-dimensional "bulk."[7] None of this has been experimentally confirmed, and all of it falls into the category of scientifically-informed speculation, but—importantly—while none of these scenarios can be demonstrated to be true, neither can they be ruled out. We may, or may not, live in a multiverse of one kind or another. The question is wide open.

How we understand Premise 2, then, depends critically on what we mean by "universe."

If we read Premise 2 to mean "the observable universe began to exist," it amounts to a vaguely-worded scientific hypothesis. It appears to be a *very approximately* correct description of the Big Bang, with the major caveat that the first moments of the Big Bang remain inscrutable. But that doesn't buy us any metaphysical knowledge, given the possibility that our universe may be part of an unknowably larger ensemble of universes. Whether that *ensemble* of universes "began to exist," or what that might mean, is anybody's guess.

Premise 2 gets us to the desired conclusion only if we read "universe" to mean "all that exists, or has ever existed, or will ever exist, no matter how ontologically distant," including the understanding that there may be self-contained universes that are inherently unobservable and very different from our own. But once we acknowledge that possibility, we lose the degree of certainty Premise 2 requires.

In other words, neither George Lemaître's theory nor Edwin Hubble's observations can buy us reliable knowledge about metaphysical reality. Pius XII's triumphalism was premature, at best.

* * *

By this point it should be obvious that the initial conclusion of the Kalam Cosmological Argument—that the universe had a cause—is, like the premises that precede it, another metaphysical assertion. It doesn't follow from any scientifically grounded reading of the first two premises; it follows only if the first two premises are established metaphysical truths. The aim of the argument is to dispel uncertainty about the existence of God by grounding that claim in less controversial propositions, but all it achieves is to distribute the uncertainty of the conclusion across two other, equally unverifiable, metaphysical assertions. So with that in mind, let's ask some better questions.

Do I know that "everything that begins to exist has a cause"?

No, I don't. (Do you?)

Do I know that "the universe (in the relevant sense) began to exist"?

No, I don't. (Do you?)

Can I conclude, then, that "the universe (in the relevant sense) has a cause"?

No, I can't. (Can you?)

* * *

There are other equally venerable arguments for the existence of God. Thomas Aquinas in his *Summa Theologica* proposed "Five Ways," many of which are approximately cosmological arguments, and all of which depend on metaphysical assertions of one sort or another to buttress their conclusions. The contemporary Catholic philosopher Edward Feser updated the Five Ways in his recent *Five Proofs of the Existence of God*, all of which are also grounded in metaphysical assertions. And there are other families of arguments for theism: arguments from objective morality, arguments from the nature of consciousness, and so on. There is nothing wrong with any of this, if we keep in mind that what's going on is a kind of systematic speculation. It may be fascinating, it may even be wise, but as Peter van Inwagen reminds us, it produces "no established body of metaphysical results."

Which raises yet another question: Why are we talking about metaphysics at all?

In a sense, it's unavoidable. Most of the major contemporary world religions, and conspicuously the Abrahamic faiths (Judaism, Christianity, and Islam), are systems of *metaphysical gnosticism*— they proclaim as truth and teach as doctrine detailed assertions of metaphysical knowledge. Other religious traditions may make less sweeping claims. The catalog of classical Greek deities and semi-divine beings is lengthy, for example, but few of those beings seemed to depend for their existence on, or care very much about, any particular conception of the nature of reality. In many indigenous religious traditions the gods are viewed as obviously active in the world, often physically embodied, amenable to praise, and jealous of their rivals. They govern the change of seasons, the success or failure of crops, the health of individuals and communities, and the maintenance of hierarchical power. Far from being any kind of *deus absconditus*, such gods are often fully present in the material world and eager to be noticed. And the belief in the existence of such beings, far from being exceptional, forms a significant part of our human cultural and intellectual heritage.

So how did the God of Christianity become a purely metaphysical being? And if the Christian God is distinctly different from Zeus and Pan and Osiris and Aten, are there any principled grounds on which an atheist can deny the existence of *all* of them?

3

A Natural History of Two Worlds

A day may come when the great beasts of the past will leap to life again in our imaginations, when we shall walk again in vanished scenes, stretch painted limbs we thought were dust, and feel again the sunshine of a million years ago.

—H. G. Wells

The early works of H. G. Wells stand at the foundation of modern English-language science fiction. Wells wasn't the first author to write imaginatively about scientific knowledge and its consequences—there are plenty of antecedents, including Mary Shelley's philosophically-minded horror story *Frankenstein*—but the genre that grew up in the pages of mainly American pulp magazines over the course of the twentieth century was indebted to Wells in countless ways. In novels and stories like *The Time Machine* and *The War of the Worlds*, Wells found a way to imaginatively inhabit the great discoveries and controversies of his time—the age and geological history of the Earth, the evolution of life, the purpose and potential of technological progress. And while the genre of fiction he inspired was often less thoughtful and insightful than his own work, science fiction continued to track and reflect a popular fascination with science and technology in an age of continuously startling new advances.

The cornerstone of all the imaginative stories Wells produced is *The Time Machine*, a short novel in which Wells managed to render nineteenth-century geological and evolutionary science as individualized human drama. In *The Time Machine* Wells turns the fate of the Earth and the evolutionary future of our species into the lived experience of a time-traveling London experimenter who has discovered a way to navigate the Fourth Dimension. ("Scientific people," Wells's protagonist says, "know very well that Time is only a kind of Space.") His time traveler eventually arrives in "the year Eight Hundred and Two Thousand Seven Hundred and One A.D.," a time when humanity has diverged into two distinct species and the planet has become a decayed utopia in which the peaceful Eloi pay for their paradisiacal existence by submitting to the appetites of their cannibalistic cousins, the Morlocks. But one of the most striking set pieces in the narrative takes place near the end of the story, when the time traveler pushes on into an even more remote future. Here the Earth is a dying and nearly lifeless planet, the sun a swollen, ancient star:

> So I travelled, stopping ever and again, in great strides of a thousand years or more, drawn on by the mystery of the earth's fate, watching with a strange fascination the sun grow larger and duller in the westward sky, and the life of the old earth ebb away. At last, more than thirty million years hence, the huge red-hot dome of the sun had come to obscure nearly a tenth part of the darkling heavens. Then I stopped once more.... A bitter cold assailed me. Rare white flakes ever and again came eddying down. To the north-eastward, the glare of snow lay under the starlight of the sable sky, and I could see an undulating

crest of hillocks pinkish white. There were fringes of ice along the sea margin, with drifting masses further out; but the main expanse of that salt ocean, all bloody under the eternal sunset, was still unfrozen.[1]

What is especially striking about this is the blunt vision of the planet we live on—its seas, its sky, its mountains and valleys—as mutable, contingent, and ultimately mortal. It's a vision that was as startling to the nineteenth century as the idea of an expanding universe was to the twentieth. Over the course of the century Wells had been born into, estimates of the age of the Earth based on Biblical scholarship—a famous example is Bishop James Ussher's calculation that the world was created on the evening of October 22, 4004 BC—had given way to Lord Kelvin's argument that the Earth must be between 20 million and 400 million years old, which in turn was revealed as a dramatic underestimate. At the same time, Christian narratives about human descent had begun to yield, if grudgingly and incompletely, to a consensus that *Homo sapiens* is an evolved and evolving species, closely related to other primates and distantly related to literally every other living thing on the planet. No scientific discovery in our own century has overturned deeply-held beliefs and widely-held preconceptions as dramatically as the constellation of scientific advances between the publication of Darwin's *On the Origin of Species* in 1859 and the detonation of the first atomic bomb in New Mexico in the summer of 1945. And it wasn't just Wells and the science fiction writers who followed him whose literary work tracked that intellectual revolution and its implications. Matthew Arnold's 1867 poem "Dover Beach" laments what Arnold saw as an ineluctable disenchantment of the world and a tragic loss of religious certainty:

The sea of faith
Was once, too, at the full, and round earth's shore
Lay like the folds of a bright girdle furl'd;

But now I only hear
Its melancholy, long, withdrawing roar,
Retreating to the breath
Of the night-wind, down the vast edges drear
And naked shingles of the world

. . .

for the world, which seems
To lie before us like a land of dreams,
So various, so beautiful, so new,
Hath really neither joy, nor love, nor light,
Nor certitude, nor peace, nor help for pain;
And we are here as on a darkling plain
Swept with confused alarms of struggle and flight,
Where ignorant armies clash by night.

And there is an echo, 78 years later, of Arnold's shattered illusions in the physicist J. Robert Oppenheimer's reaction as he watched the fireball and mushroom cloud of the Trinity atomic bomb test boil into the sky above the Jornada del Muerto desert: "Now I am become Death," he thought bleakly, "the destroyer of worlds," a quotation from the Bhagavad Gita.

Projecting a somewhat more optimistic version of the scientific vision of the world into the future became a bread-and-butter strategy for twentieth-century science fiction writers. Less commonly, Wells and his literary descendants have made occasional sojourns into our deep evolutionary and geological past. The time traveler in the prehistoric world is something of a cliché now—recall Ray Bradbury's "The Sound of Thunder," in which a tourist stepping on a butterfly in the Late Cretaceous alters modern history in a dismaying fashion—but only rarely have writers attempted to cast our ancient ancestors as protagonists. Wells did so twice, once in a sketch called "The Grisly Folk," and once in a longer narrative called "A Story of the Stone Age" (which he bracketed with a parallel narrative, "A Story of the Days to Come").

How our Paleolithic ancestors have been portrayed in fiction depends in turn on what paleontologists and anthropologists have believed about them. In "The Grisly Folk", Homo sapiens and Homo neanderthalensis are locked in a brutal struggle for mastery of Ice Age Europe. "Hairy or grisly, with a big face like a mask, great brow ridges and no forehead, clutching an enormous flint and running like a baboon, with his head forward and not like a man with his head up," Wells wrote, the Neanderthal "must have been a fearsome creature for our forefathers to come upon." It's easy and probably correct to read elements of colonialism and racism into Wells's portrayal of our Neanderthal cousins. Scholars of Wells's generation, like the Egyptologist Sir Flinders Petrie, created "[h]ierarchies of anatomical and cultural advancement in past peoples" writes the archeologist Rebecca Wragg Sykes, which "directly fed poisonous notions of competition and racial purity that were foundational in eugenics [and were] reflected in some fiction, such as H. G. Wells' 1921 *The Grisly Folk*, which subtly positions the eradication of an almost parasitic, animalistic hominin race as vital to human survival."[2] In this story Wells gives the "true men," as he calls them, no religion worth mentioning. The Neanderthals in his vision are far too animalistic for the question even to apply, and in any case the "true men" soon drove them to extinction.

Wells's other work of fiction about our ancestors, "A Story of the Stone Age," is a longer and more charitable narrative. Its setting is "a time beyond the memory of man ... a time when one might have walked dryshod from France (as we call it now) to England, and when a broad and sluggish Thames flowed through its marshes to meet its father Rhine, flowing through a wide and level country that is underwater in these latter days.... In that remote age the valley which runs along the foot of the Downs did not exist, and the south of Surrey was a range of hills, fir-clad on the middle slopes, and snow-capped for the better part of the year." Wells's main characters, the young Paleolithic couple Ugh-lomi and Eudena, are sympathetically drawn, but their religious thought is still portrayed as little more than a kind of vague animism.

It is of course nearly impossible for anthropologists (or even writers of fiction) to authentically recreate the mind-set of our earliest ancestors and related hominin species, for the simple reason that beliefs don't leave fossils and the spoken word vanishes like smoke into the air. The best we can do is to draw inferences from the scanty evidence we have of their behavior. And as that evidence has slowly accumulated—and as paleontologists and anthropologists have learned to examine their own biases—a more nuanced depiction of our cousins and ancestors has begun to emerge.

That nuanced depiction is reflected in the paleontological fiction that has appeared since Wells, including Jean M. Auel's bestselling series beginning with *Clan of the Cave Bear* (1980), Stephen Baxter's 2003 novel *Evolution*, and a recent book by Kim Stanley Robinson, *Shaman* (2013), to date probably the most well-informed and carefully-written attempt to imagine life in the late Pleistocene era some 30,000 years ago. Robinson in particular does a fine job of depicting what might be called the proto-religiosity of his early humans, centered around questions of life and death, the flickering torch-lit spaces of natural caves, the potency of art, and the ubiquity and significance of dreams and visions.

And there has been a great deal of recent research that helps illuminate our understanding of human life in the late Pleistocene. At a Paleolithic site called Sunghir in modern Russia, two boys were buried by their tribesmen in graves filled with "more than 10,000 mammoth ivory beads, more than 20 armbands, about 300 pierced fox teeth, 16 ivory mammoth spears, carved artwork, deer antlers and two human fibulas (calf bones) laid across the boys' chests."[3] Much remains speculative, but the presence of grave goods at these and other such sites suggests that a kind of ceremonial religiosity surrounding death is not only deeply embedded in early human culture but was something we may have shared with our not-quite-human cousins. A Neanderthal site at the Shanidar caves in northern Iraq has revealed deliberately buried bodies, in graves that might have been strewn with flowers, though that claim is controversial.

And given the wide latitude for speculation that follows from relatively scant evidence, some anthropologists (and atheists) have offered suggestions about the origins of religion in human prehistory. Cognitive anthropologist Pascal Boyer, in his book *Religion Explained: The Evolutionary Origins of Religious Thought* (2001), acknowledges the power and persistence of religion and finds an explanation, or at least a significant part of the explanation, in human cognitive processes and their idiosyncrasies. Boyer dismisses the commonly proposed "functionalist" explanations for the invention of religion—that it explains what our ancestors couldn't understand, that it provides comfort in the face of grief or loss, or that it creates and reinforces social order—as inadequate, and he is equally dismissive of the idea that religion is just a symptom of human gullibility. "The sleep of reason is no explanation for religion as it is," Boyer writes. "There are many possible unsupported claims and only a few religious themes. . . . We should understand what makes human minds so selective in what supernatural claims they find plausible."

Any brief summary of Boyer's thought risks oversimplifying it, but his own summation contains this paragraph:

> For eons, people have naturally talked about millions of exceedingly parochial and contextual matters but also about some objects and things that are not directly observable. . . . Among the millions of messages exchanged, some are attention-grabbing because they violate intuitions about objects and beings in our environment. These counterintuitive descriptions have a certain staying power, as memory experiments suggest. . . . Some of these themes are particularly salient because they are about agents.[4]

"Agents," in this context, refers to beings capable of taking deliberate actions in the observable world, and we "infer agency" whenever we attribute some event to a deliberative cause—the intuition that a rustling of leaves, say, is due to a stalking predator or a child climbing a tree. As the British philosopher A. C. Grayling writes,

> The picture that emerges is that religion stems from the period when stories, myths and supernatural beliefs served as, in effect, mankind's earliest science and technology. To the inhabitants of such a culture, natural phenomena are most intuitively explained by seeing them as the work of purposive agents who variously cause the wind to blow and the rain to fall, whose footsteps on the cloud are thunderous, and who are responsible for the cycling of the stars and the growth of vegetation in springtime.[5]

Not all "agency detection" explanations for the origins of religious belief are alike, but what they have in common is that they place responsibility for such beliefs on a cognitive failure of one kind or another, either in misattributing agency or in preferring agency explanations over better but less intriguing stories. We are religious, it would seem, because our cognitive abilities are frail and easily misled. Reason is held hostage by our evolutionary history; more perfect thinkers would never have entertained such irrational ideas in the first place.

That's plausible, but might there be an explanation less unflattering to the cognitive skills of our ancestors or ourselves? What if the intuitions of our earliest forebears were *not* irrational? Grayling hints at such a possibility when he says of our ancestors that they "could feel themselves to be causes of events.... How could things happen in nature unless caused, and how caused unless by an agent? It is a simple argument by analogy from their own case, and as such it is an empirical argument."[6]

That's better, but perhaps we can do better still. Our ancestors' intuitions were obviously not formal philosophical arguments. As

H. G. Wells says of his Paleolithic protagonist in "A Story of the Stone Age," he "made no philosophical deductions, but he perceived the thing was so." But that doesn't mean they might not be entirely rational. Let's set aside agency detection, and instead consider two related concepts that are plausibly very ancient:

1. There are two worlds, a daylight world and a shadow world; the two worlds are divided by a border, but the border is permeable; entities native to one world may sometimes pass into the other; and,

2. I am a spirit inside a body, but I am not the same as my body and I am not always confined to my body.

* * *

Are these irrational beliefs, or are they reasonable intuitions? Consider the first proposition:

> *There are two worlds, a daylight world and a shadow world;*
> *the two worlds are divided by a border,*
> *but the border is permeable; entities native to one world*
> *may sometimes pass into the other.*

Could this be, as A. C. Grayling says, an "empirical argument"—or at least an intuition drawn from common experience?

Picture a Paleolithic ancestor of ours—let's say, a woman living in southern Europe at the end of the Ice Age some thirty thousand years ago. We can call her Eudena, after the female protagonist of "A Story of the Stone Age." Summoned to the present—maybe she hitched a ride on Wells's Time Machine—and equipped with the equivalent of *Star Trek*'s universal translator, would Eudena be able to defend her belief on empirical grounds, that is, by presenting evidence?

"It's just the way of things," Eudena might answer. "Isn't it obvious to you? By day, when we're awake, the world is easy to know. We know how to follow the ibex; we know where to find shellfish on the tidal flats; we trade with the people upriver. But when we're asleep we travel differently. Our bodies lie motionless, but we move in the shadow world. Sometimes we speak to the dead. Sometimes we find ourselves in strange places. And sleeping is not the only way into that world. Fevers, or fasting, or certain plants, can take a person there. How do you not know this? Even the tall, pale people you call Neanderthals know this. We know it without speaking about it. It's just a true thing. When people lie still at night, they travel in the shadow world. And when they die and lie still forever, the shadow world is where they go. I've seen them there myself."

Notice that Eudena isn't making anything like what we would today call a metaphysical claim. That distinction, like the distinction between "natural" and "supernatural," is foreign to her. All of what she says is evidential, drawn from common experience. The existence of the shadow world isn't a hypothesis; she's been there, and so have her friends and family. Her vocabulary for describing dreams and visionary experiences isn't the vocabulary we might use, but it maps neatly onto our own experience, thirty thousand years later. Like Eudena, I have encountered the dead in my dreams—most often my father, who died when I was nineteen years old and who still occasionally appears, in contexts that are sometimes comforting, sometimes frightening. From our place in the twenty-first century we might argue that these apparitions aren't "real," but that's another distinction Eudena has no reason to make. These are simply her experiences, one as real as the next.

Notice, too, that Eudena doesn't seem to think she has been *taught* this knowledge about the daylight and the shadow worlds. It seems to her self-evident, and perhaps it is. The experience of dreaming and waking is a human universal, and it may well have existed in us even before our capacity for language was fully developed. She didn't invent the idea of the shadow world. The idea is reflected or implied in many of the cultural artifacts that have survived from Eudena's day to ours. Perhaps other hominin species shared the same intuition, whether or not they were able to articulate it.

We might guess that Eudena has additional ideas about the daylight and the shadow worlds, ideas that are more specific and less well-evidenced. Maybe she believes certain people can influence the entities that inhabit the shadow world, bringing good or ill fortune to the band of humans to which she belongs. Maybe she believes that such people can cure illness or foretell the future. These ideas are cultural accretions, in the sense that Eudena learned them from those around her; they are particular to her community, and other human communities might have had similar but distinctly different beliefs. But the core concept of the two worlds is experiential. Only its interpretation is culturally created and transmitted.

The same is true of the second assertion: *I am a spirit inside a body, but I am not the same as my body and I am not always confined to my body.* Again, for Eudena, this is not a "belief" but a daily lived experience, and she finds herself puzzled and a little exasperated by our curiosity about it:

"Do you people not sleep? Last night I slept and went to a dark place where my mother was surrounded by wolves. I was there with her—I spoke to her—but my people tell me my body never left the camp. What traveled, if not the part of me that isn't my body?"

* * *

If we want to talk about Eudena's intuitions concisely, we'll need to name them. The first intuition—*there are two worlds, a daylight world and a shadow world; the two worlds are divided by a border, but the border is permeable; entities native to one world may sometimes pass into the other*—we'll call *dual ontology*. (The word "ontology" has many definitions, but I'm using it here to mean "a particular theory about the nature of being or the kinds of things that have existence," quoting the Merriam-Webster dictionary.)

The second intuition—*I am a spirit inside a body, but I am not the same as my body and I am not always confined to my body*—we'll call *the disembodied self.*

We have identified these as, at least for Eudena, rational inferences from daily experience, which means they are no more intrinsically "religious" than any other inference we might draw from life. But when we examine them in the light of human history, three observations stand out:

1. Dual ontology and the disembodied self are persistent and ubiquitous intuitions, across cultures and across time;

2. Although neither intuition is itself "religious," any cultural product that accretes around it—any formalized or specified description of the shadow world, any propitiatory sacrifice or other ritual intended to summon, placate, supplicate, or defend against its inhabitants, any demarcation of a class of people deemed uniquely able to interpret or conduct journeys of the disembodied self—all of these look very much like religion in the broadest sense of the word. And,

3. These intuitions, although they are entirely rational from Eudena's point of view, are mistaken.

4

The Door in the Wall

Late in the nineteenth century, in the West Kensington district of London, a boy, not yet six years old, walks past a green door in a white wall.

The boy—his mother deceased, his father an inattentive and preoccupied lawyer—is accustomed to wandering freely through the neighborhood. He encounters the green door in an unfamiliar but otherwise unexceptional street. The door, surrounded by shabby storefronts, is unmarked, but something about it attracts the boy's attention. It seems both inviting and somehow dangerous. He passes it, hesitates, turns back, and, finally, on an impulse, opens the door and steps through.

He finds himself in a vast garden, full of light, inhabited by benevolent creatures—a pair of friendly panthers; a young woman who guides him and offers cryptic answers to his questions; nameless playmates with whom he enjoys fascinating games. The garden is immense: "it stretched far and wide, this way and that. I believe there were hills far away. Heaven knows where West Kensington had suddenly got to. . . . I became in a moment a very glad and wonder-happy little boy—in another world."

The young woman eventually shows the boy a book in which the events of his life are inscribed, including this visit to the garden, but when he tries to turn the page and learn his future he abruptly finds himself back on "a long gray street in West Kensington, in that chill hour of afternoon before the lamps are lit."

The boy knows, somehow, that he won't be able to find the door again even if he sets out to look for it. But a few years later, the green door finds him. As an adolescent hunting for a shortcut on the way to school, he passes the door once again. This time he doesn't immediately open it. Now that he knows where it is, he reasons, he can come back later. He's confident enough that he brags to his friends about the miraculous door, and when they mock him he offers to lead them there. But when he tries to do so, he loses his way. The route he followed seems to no longer exist; the green door is gone.

He sees the door again from a horse-drawn cab on his way to the University of Oxford, where he has won a scholarship, but he is afraid of being late and losing his position, and he doesn't ask the cabbie to stop. Years later, in the midst of a successful career, he catches sight of the door yet again, in a different location, and again fails to open it.

More years later, the door is barely a memory, but "recently it has come back to me. With it there has come a sense as though some thin tarnish had spread itself over my world. I began to think of it as a sorrowful and bitter thing that I should never see that door again."

Soon after, the man's lifeless body is found in an excavation near East Kensington Station. The pit where he fell is protected by "a hoarding upon the high-road, in which a small doorway has been cut for the convenience of some of the workmen who live in that direction." The access door was left unfastened, and the man, stepping through it, has fallen to his death.

* * *

The story summarized here is "The Door in the Wall," by H. G. Wells. It's one of his most reprinted works of short fiction, in part because it succeeds in so many different ways: as a moody depiction of childhood loneliness; as a metaphor for the seductive allure of the imagination; as an illustration of the way the minutiae of adult life distract us from deeper feelings; as a portrait of the human longing for a Utopia that continually retreats beyond the horizon of practical possibility. For its length, the story has more light and darkness in it than some of us manage to pack into a hefty novel.

But for our purposes, we can look at it as a working model of a dual ontology.

There are two worlds in the Wells story, the dully ordinary daylight world and the indefinitely extensive, deeply alluring garden beyond the wall. The two worlds are divided by a border—the wall—but the border is permeable; there is a door, if you know where to find it (or if it knows where to find you). Some entities are native to the daylight world, including human beings. Some entities are native to the garden, like the friendly panthers or the protagonist's nameless playmates.

The story is fantasy, of course, but it's remarkable how easily we accept its fantastic premise and how effortlessly we suspend our disbelief—perhaps because it fits the template of dual ontology so neatly. And if we begin to look for examples of dual ontology elsewhere in contemporary popular culture, they're not hard to find. Kansas shares a border with the shadow world of Oz. Narnia is accessible by way of a wardrobe in an English country house. If you want to go to Hogwarts, head for Platform 9¾. Robert A. Heinlein's novel *Glory Road* begins, "I know a place where there is no smog and no parking problem and no population explosion . . . no Cold War and no H-bombs and no television commercials. . . . The climate is the sort that Florida and California claim (and neither has), the land is lovely, the people are friendly and hospitable to strangers. . . ."[1] No ordinary compass will guide you to these places. They're east of the sun and west of the moon. They are, like the mirage of a hovering city in Ray Bradbury's story "A Miracle of Rare Device," elusive, "now shimmered by heat, now threatening to blow away forever."[2]

Folklore and indigenous religions worldwide provide countless other examples. In the Shinto tradition, our human world (*Utsushi-yo*) is bordered above by the Plain of High Heaven (*Takama-no-hara*) and below by the Nether World (*Yomotsu-kuni*). According to Michael Ashkenazi's *Handbook of Japanese Mythology*, "Two significant features [in the Plain of High Heaven] are its exits. There is the Heavenly Floating Bridge, often identified with the Milky Way, which joins heaven to earth. There is also a major crossroads, of which one road leads to heaven, the other to earth."[3] Shinto cosmology is vastly more complicated than that, of course, and so are the cosmologies of indigenous cultures worldwide, but dual ontologies—in the sense that the human world is said to co-exist with other inhabited worlds that are partially accessible but distinctly separate from it—are an easily-identified recurring feature.

But the shadow world isn't necessarily a happy place, and its inhabitants don't always visit us for benign reasons. Another iconic story: In Washington, D.C., not far from the campus of Georgetown University, a woman, an actor currently separated from her husband, is living with her 11-year-old daughter. After the girl finds a Ouija board in the basement of their townhouse and begins to play with it, the child's behavior changes in alarming ways. Normally outgoing and friendly, the girl becomes withdrawn, frightened, hostile, aggressive. As the symptoms worsen, her mother seeks medical and psychiatric help, but the child's condition continues to decline and her symptoms grow more dismaying, even terrifying. Her bed shakes, her skin is disfigured, she displays unusual strength. She seems to know more than she ought to. She speaks (and curses) in languages she hasn't learned. These increasingly inexplicable pathologies lead the child's desperate mother to seek help from a pair of Catholic priests, who diagnose demonic possession and agree to attempt an exorcism. In the denouement—spoiler alert—one of the priests dies during the harrowing ritual, while the other invites the demon to possess him and then leaps to his death in an act of heroic self-sacrifice, recovering his fragile faith in God even as he draws his last breath.

The story is, of course, *The Exorcist*. William Peter Blatty's 1971 novel sold out multiple printings, and the movie based on it, directed by William Friedkin, terrified its audiences so effectively that in 1975 *The Journal of Nervous and Mental Disease* published an article called "Cinematic neurosis following 'The Exorcist': Report of four cases." The book and movie both draw on traditional Catholic theology and demonology. "Being a Catholic," one character in the novel says, "I believe that we all have a foot in two worlds."

Pazuzu—the demon named in the novel—is not native to our daylight world, but he crosses the border between worlds as a disembodied self who takes up residence in the body of a young girl. That readers of the book and audiences for the movie found the premise so persuasive is more evidence that the ideas of dual ontology and the disembodied self are never far from our minds. But if these ideas are so commonplace, so apparently plausible, and have their roots in a rational inference from human experience, how can we be sure they're wrong?

* * *

The culturally-specific beliefs and practices that accrete around these simple ideas inevitably face at least four hazards: time, geography, astronomy, and geology.

Time is an obvious one. Human culture is elastic. Rituals evolve, interpretations mutate. The hierarchies that administer rites and define beliefs change with every generation and may, from time to time, be overthrown and replaced. The history of religion is a record of such gradual and sudden shifts. The old gods are scorned by an ambitious Pharaoh, and for a time, Aten rules the cosmos; the old gods return under a new ruler, and Isis and Osiris are worshipped once again; eventually foreign gods arrive to displace Isis and Osiris, whose temples crumble to ruins—and so it goes. All human beliefs are subject to change, and most human beliefs are at least to some extent constrained by common experience, but the specific beliefs that accrete around dual ontology and the disembodied self are *less* constrained by experience and *more* susceptible to change than most other beliefs. Our belief that the seasons cycle in regular procession is sturdy, in part because it is renewed and reinforced by direct experience, year after year. But our belief that the weather is ruled by the Theoi Ouranioi is intrinsically more fragile. If it goes away, as it has gone away in the modern world, nothing perceptible is changed.

Time threatens fixed religious beliefs in other ways. When a cultural context shifts, as when previously isolated communities mingle or conduct trade or go to war, religious beliefs are as susceptible to exchange or extinction as any other cultural product. When religions merge and borrow elements from one another, we call the resulting new belief systems *syncretic*. Again, what is at stake is not the core notion of dual ontology and the disembodied self but the culturally-specific elaborations of these ideas. The complex Mesopotamian pantheon of divine beings is today neglected by everyone but the scholars and historians who preserve its memory, and no one in the modern world attributes any real power to those beings—unless you want to count the Mesopotamian god Pazuzu, recruited to play the incorporeal villain in *The Exorcist*. Pascal Boyer in *Religion Explained* observes that religious concepts often migrate from "serious" to "nonserious" modes. Pazuzu, no longer feared for his power to wield storms and inflict drought, is reduced to sneaking into a Georgetown rental by way of the Ouija board in the basement. Thor, exiled from Valhalla, becomes an amiable dude played by Chris Hemsworth in a Marvel movie. Time can be merciless to the gods.

The remaining categories amount to versions of evidential disconfirmation. An example of disconfirmation familiar to all of us is the Genesis story of Adam and Eve, any literal interpretation of which has been discredited by more than one branch of modern science. But evidential disconfirmation isn't something Charles Darwin invented. Whenever a religious system places a shadow world at a specified time or place, it runs the risk of being falsified by new evidence.

If the shadow world is said to be on earth but beyond any known or well-traveled territory, that belief risks disconfirmation by *geography*—that is, by the increasingly accurate mapping of the daylight world. In classical Greek mythology, the Isles of the Blessed (aka the Elysian Fields or Elysium) were a paradisiacal place where dead heroes or other mortals chosen by the gods retired to spend an idyllic afterlife. "No snow is there," according to Homer, "nor heavy storm, nor ever rain, but ever does Ocean send up blasts of the shrill-blowing West Wind that they may give cooling to men."[4] There, according to the Greek poet Hesiod, the deceased "live untouched by sorrow ... happy heroes for whom the grain-giving earth bears honey-sweet fruit flourishing thrice a year."[5] The Isles of the Blessed were alleged to have a specific location, and classical sources were often fairly explicit about it. The Greek historian Plutarch, who denied the truth of the Homeric myths about Elysium, nevertheless says the Isles are "two in number, separated by a very narrow strait; they are ten thousand furlongs distant from Africa.... They enjoy moderate rains at long intervals, and winds which for the most part are soft and precipitate dews, so that the islands not only have a rich soil which is excellent for plowing and planting, but also produce a natural fruit that is plentiful and wholesome enough to feed, without toil or trouble, a leisured folk."[6] *Book me a ticket*, you might think. Alas, the gradual expansion of geographic knowledge has caused the Isles of the Blessed to evaporate like a precipitated dew on a sunny morning.

Other classical and folkloric traditions identify a shadow world located under the surface of the earth, often a drear, unpleasant place associated with the dead. To whatever degree these beliefs are literalized, they are subject to disconfirmation by *geology*. The Greek Hades is a familiar example, but underworld journeys are common in many other traditions. Underworlds where dead souls dwell feature in Zulu, Bantu, and Ashanti stories, for instance. In Chinese popular religion, souls in the underworld are tried by the Ten Judges prior to their reincarnation. The idea of a land beneath the earth isn't intrinsically absurd, and the notion that the earth might have a hollow and inhabitable interior, if not one occupied by the souls of the dead, seemed at least remotely plausible as recently as the nineteenth century. John Cleeve Symes, an American Army officer, argued in 1818 that an inner world below the earth might be accessible through openings at the north and south poles, and Jeremiah N. Reynolds, a newspaper editor who joined Symes on the lecture circuit, proposed fitting out an expedition to the South Pole to search for it. Cleeve was wrong, but his and similar ideas were popular enough to inspire Edgar Allan Poe's novel *The Narrative of Arthur Gordon Pym* (1838) and Jules Verne's *Journey to the Center of the Earth* (1867), in which the protagonists discover dinosaurs roaming the underworld. But by the mid-twentieth century, the poles had been mapped, the folkloric caverns had all been explored, and our understanding of the geology of the earth's crust left no room for Homer's dead souls or Verne's living dinosaurs.

Astronomy is an obvious mode of disconfirmation for religious cosmologies. We don't refer to the sky as "the heavens" without reason. Biblical cosmology, like the Babylonian cosmology from which it drew many elements, envisioned a world divided between the underworld, the earth, and the heavens above; with the influence of Greek thought this evolved into a model of the earth as spherical and surrounded by a number of concentric "heavens" in which various entities were said to dwell. English-speakers still use the phrase "seventh heaven" to mean ultimate happiness, and you might still occasionally hear the sky called "the firmament." "Thus God made the firmament," according to Genesis, "and divided the waters which were under the firmament from the waters which were above the firmament; and it was so. And God called the firmament Heaven."

The science fiction writer Ted Chiang is probably best known for the novelette "Story of Your Life," on which the 2016 film *Arrival* was based, but one of his earliest and most memorable short stories is "Tower of Babylon," which literalizes the Biblical story of the Tower of Babel. "Tower of Babylon" is told from the point of view of Hillalum, a miner who has been hired to work atop an immensely tall tower that has been under construction for many years and has finally grown high enough to touch the Vault of Heaven, the solid dome above the earth. Hillalum has been tasked to help finish the project: to dig through the Vault to reach whatever lies on the other side. The story inhabits Biblical cosmology as if it were solemn fact, never stepping outside its own premise. In other words, this is how the world might have been if Biblical cosmology had *not* been disconfirmed. We read it from our contemporary perspective as pure fantasy, but to a literate Judean of 500 BC the story might have seemed more like . . . well, science fiction.

Hillalum performs his work diligently, eventually tunneling through the Vault to the other side. A torrent of water floods the hole he has opened in the bottom of heaven, nearly drowning him, but he survives without being washed away and emerges from the Vault into a surprisingly ordinary-seeming landscape. "[T]he foothills of some mountains, and rock and sand stretched to the horizon. . . . Was heaven just like the earth? Did Yahweh dwell in a place such as this? Or was this merely another realm within

Yahweh's Creation, another earth above his own, while Yahweh dwelled still higher?"

But it's neither. The truth is even stranger than that. "He had climbed above the reservoirs of heaven, and arrived back at the earth." The cosmos, it seems, has the closed geometry of a Moebius strip. "It was clear now why Yahweh had not struck down the tower, had not punished men for wishing to reach beyond the bounds set for them, for the longest journey would merely return them to the place where they'd come. . . . By this construction, Yahweh's work was indicated, and Yahweh's work was concealed."[7]

Even in this meticulously literalized alternate cosmology, the shadow world retreats beyond the borders of the known.

* * *

Anything we add to Eudena's intuition, any ostensible map of the shadow world, makes it vulnerable to disconfirmation. At one time in human history it was easy enough to locate the shadow world and its inhabitants somewhere safely out of sight—beyond the horizon, in the deeps of the earth, on a mountaintop, in the sky itself—without fear of contradiction. But the steady accumulation of human knowledge has made that maneuver vastly more difficult. When we talk about religion (in the broadest sense) being eroded by science (in the broadest sense), this is usually what we mean.

But what about Eudena's intuition in its simplest form? *There are two worlds, a daylight world and a shadow world; the two worlds are divided by a border, but the border is permeable; entities native to one world may sometimes pass into the other.* Could even that minimal version be subject to disconfirmation?

Eudena's intuition has a few moving parts, and each rests to some degree on the others, so let's do a little deconstruction.

To begin with, what do we mean by "worlds"? As we've mentioned, contemporary physics has postulated (but not evidentially confirmed) the existence of multiple universes of various descriptions. Could one of these be where the gods live? But a multiverse, if it exists, can't rescue Eudena's intuition, because these other universes are causally disconnected from ours—they have either branched from it in the past or were never causally connected with it to begin with. What happens in the universe next door, stays in the universe next door. There may be a Wall, but there is no Door.

The best candidate for a material shadow world might be dark matter, the hypothetical weakly-interacting particles physicists have invoked to explain the motion of galaxies and other anomalous observations. If more than one kind of dark matter particle exists, and if these particles are able to interact with one another, they might plausibly combine to create dark planets, dark stars, or other complex objects—objectively real places we could detect only through their gravitational influence. The Wall in this case is their near absence of interaction with ordinary matter, and the Door is the detectable influence of their gravity. A kind of counter-universe that surrounds us, is invisible to us, perhaps passes through us without touching us, and is imperceptible except on a scale so large that we can detect It only by its ethereal tug on vast congregations of stars—could that be a candidate for Eudena's shadow world? But no, even that won't do. Dark matter worlds, if such things exist, don't share a navigable border with our daily existence—and for Eudena's intuition to be meaningful, the shadow world must be inhabited and entities from the shadow world must somehow manifest themselves to human beings in a perceptible way. And that's not what we find. Dark matter doesn't interact with the electromagnetic field, but the gods do—they must, in fact, if they want to affect the weather, appear to mortal eyes, or intervene in human thought. To serve as Eudena's shadow world, dark matter would have to act in precisely the ways it is defined as *not* acting.

To say this more explicitly: there is no evidence for the existence of a detectible dual ontology in our current understanding of the observable universe.

In the face of that, is there any way to protect a robust dual ontology from disconfirmation? The traditional strategy has been to push the shadow world out of the known and into the unknown, and the surest way to do that is to exclude it from the observable universe entirely. If we define the entirety of the observable universe as "nature," then the shadow world must be something altogether else. The consequence of this idea is that reality cleaves into two fractions, "the natural" and the "the supernatural"—ordinarily distinct, but occasionally intermingled.

But that doesn't protect Eudena's intuition, it simply restates it. The distinction between "natural" and "supernatural" makes no sense unless we're already committed to a dual ontology. In the absence of a presumed dual ontology—and a fairly highly-specified one, at that—there is no rational metric by which to distinguish objects, events, or phenomena that are "natural" from those that are "supernatural." And again, we have no compelling evidence that the observable universe is partitioned into natural and supernatural sectors.

What does that leave for the shadow world and its inhabitants? From its earliest beginnings, Christian theology has raised the possibility that the shadow world and its inhabitants might exist in the way certain immaterial "objects" like mathematical truths and geometric shapes exist in Platonic philosophy—that is, without location, without extension in time or space, not as detectible phenomena but as an eternality of truth distinct from the world of daily experience. Where, after all, does the number five live? Everywhere and nowhere. You can't touch it, you can't measure its length with a ruler, you can't calculate its radiant energy or estimate its half-life. Nevertheless, there it is, *fiveness*, implicit in the world and everywhere at once. Perhaps God exists in the same way.

But even that doesn't entirely salvage Eudena's intuition. *Fiveness* doesn't bring the rain, sanctify the priesthood, offer salvation, or tempt Jesus to throw himself from the roof of the temple to see whether the angels will bear him up. For any of these things to happen, the inhabitants of the shadow world must be unlike "five-ness" in the sense that they possess agency: a capacity to act on the observable universe and the will to do so.

But by identifying the shadow world with universal truths, Christian theology has done something distinctly different. For God, as defined in this way, to *be* God, he cannot be a partial being, responsible for just one tribe, one city, or one nation. God must be the God of *all* reality, at *all* times and *all* places, no matter how remote.

This is a bold move. We may be tempted to think of it as a retreat from the observable world into metaphysics, but from a historical perspective, it isn't a retreat at all. In many ways it's the opposite. The shadow world has stormed the castle of ultimate reality. The shadow world no longer supervenes on the observable universe; the observable universe is subordinate to, and depends for its existence on, the shadow world. Figure and ground have been utterly reversed. The shadow world is reality at its most fundamental level—our world has become the shadow world's shadow world.

Does this make the God of Christian theology something categorically different from gods like Isis and Osiris? To an extent, it does. Pagan and folkloric gods were often explicitly local, and expected to be, but the God who has been promoted to equivalence with ultimate reality can brook no such particularity. His universality is built into his definition.

But we're still right there in the familiar double ontology of Eudena's intuition. The metaphysics of Christian theology becomes, if not a physical place, at least strangely place-like. It's an abode not just for God but for other metaphysical beings—demons, angels, perhaps saints or other vagrant spirits. Passage between the two realms is exceptional, but possible; the God of foundational reality is able to beget a child with a human mother. This is still a world divided from ours by a wall with a door in it, a world inhabited by entities who are native to it and who from time to time pass through that door to intercede in our affairs.

What has changed is that, by anchoring the shadow world in fundamental reality, Christian theology has inescapably become a system of *metaphysical gnosticism*. To espouse Christianity is to explicitly claim knowledge about metaphysical reality, or to defer to those who make such claims.

* * *

George MacDonald was a nineteenth-century Christian minister who graduated from the University of Aberdeen in 1845 with a master's degree in chemistry and physics, but he is probably best remembered today as the author of a number of fantasy novels (*The Princess and the Goblin*, *At the Back of the North Wind*, and *Phantastes*, among others). His religious ideas were occasionally controversial, but his gentle piety was much admired and his writing much beloved in its day. An American lecture tour in 1872-73 played to standing-room-only audiences. Among his other claims to fame, it was MacDonald who helped convince his friend Lewis Carrol to submit *Alice's Adventures in Wonderland* for publication. His novels are still read by fantasy enthusiasts, but his most-cited work is probably the poem "Baby," with its memorable first verse:

Where did you come from, baby dear?
Out of the everywhere into the here.

Writers of all stripes have poached that verse. Isaac Asimov published a collection of essays called *Out of the Everywhere*. The science fiction writer Alice Sheldon (writing as James Tiptree Jr.) gave her 1981 short story collection the title *Out of the Everywhere and Other Extraordinary Visions*. The poem itself is a cloyingly sentimental Victorian ode to a newborn child, though I would defy any parent of a newborn, however cynical, to read it without getting at least a little misty. It's also, if you read it literally, which you probably shouldn't, a kind of Door-in-the-Wall story. Babies are assembled in the shadow world ("*Whence that three-cornered smile of bliss? / Three angels gave me at once a kiss*") and transmitted to earth. Any messy biological intermediate steps are carefully elided.

But if we want to sum up the thirty-thousand-year evolution of religious thought from Eudena's intuition to the grand abstractions of classical Christian theology, we could do worse than to paraphrase George MacDonald:

> *Where have they gone, the gods so dear?*
> *Into the Everywhere, out of the Here.*

5

Twenty Gods or No God: The Sins of Christianity

In the first quarter of the twenty-first century, science fiction is a big-money, high-stakes cultural industry—an inescapable cinematic presence, a reliable font of must-watch television, and a genre that regularly attracts city-sized populations of fans, hucksters, and industry professionals to events like San Diego's annual Comic-Con. Of a recent list of the fifty top-grossing motion pictures, at least half qualify as science fiction or fantasy. During the first year of the COVID-19 pandemic, movie studios initially believed blockbuster science fiction releases like Christopher Nolan's *Tenet* or Denis Villeneuve's *Dune* would lure audiences back to financially devastated theaters. (*Tenet* failed in that ambition, but a delayed release of *Dune* filled seats effectively as the pandemic seemed to wind down.) The same year, Chinese film authorities proposed policies aimed at boosting that country's output of science fiction movies—at least, science fiction movies that dutifully "implement Xi Jinping Thought."[1]

It was not always thus.

Anyone who has grown up in a culture so completely saturated with science fiction might find it hard to grasp what the genre
was for the majority of the twentieth century: a low-rent pulp literature with a small but fanatically loyal readership, a trivial fraction of a fiction-magazine publishing complex that had peaked
during the Depression and was, by the mid-1950s, in the process
of being gutted by the bankruptcy of its distribution networks. At
mid-century, the idea that science fiction might one day dominate
popular culture would have seemed like a joke. It *was*, in fact, a
joke: in 1956 Robert Bloch, the writer best known for his novel
Psycho, published a satirical story called "A Way of Life," about a
future in which science fiction had shaped civilization and writers
like Heinlein and Asimov were revered as heroes. The readers of
the magazine *Fantastic Universe*, where the story was first printed,
probably enjoyed a good laugh at that idea. (Elsewhere in America
circa 1956, the novel *Peyton Place* was scandalizing mainstream
readers, Elvis Presley's "Hound Dog" topped the music charts, and
President Eisenhower officially added the words "under God" to
the Pledge of Allegiance. *Fantastic Universe* went out of business
four years later.) Salvaged by the booming paperback market, elevated by occasional endorsements from public figures like the
British writer Kingsley Amis, and legitimized by the space program, by 1970 science fiction had already begun the trajectory that
would turn it into a twenty-first-century cultural behemoth. But
that exponential curve, at the time, was still just a faint uptick on
the trend-line.

It was in the 1970s that I discovered science fiction as a subculture. The science fiction fandom of the day was a microcosm in
which professional writers, would-be professionals, and dedicated
readers met and mingled at a handful of regional conventions usually attended by a couple of hundred people. It was nevertheless a
place where many writers had begun and nurtured careers, and it
was a place where I aspired to do the same. It was also an environment in which my atheism was uncontroversial.

I had been lucky that way. My immediate family had never made an issue of my atheism, mainly because I didn't talk about it. I don't think I ever used the word in front of my parents or my older siblings. That wasn't a strategy on my part; it was an unspoken household rule. We never talked about religion. Church attendance had been an inevitable and tedious Sunday ritual during my early childhood, but we left our piety at the church steps when we climbed into the Rambler for the drive home.

I don't have an easy explanation for that. My parents, and my father in particular, came from deeply religious backgrounds. My uncle Kenneth Wilson was for several years the editor of the *Christian Herald*, at the time the country's largest interdenominational Protestant monthly magazine and a citadel of conservative evangelical Christianity—although, after my uncle assumed the editorship in 1967, the magazine was chided for shifting "rather markedly toward a liberal theology and a conciliar ecumenism," according to rival publication *Christianity Today*.[2] A hint of the glamour of the New York publishing world seemed (in my eyes) to cling to my uncle Kenneth, which more than made up for any disagreement I might have imagined having with his faith, and I always looked forward to his occasional visits. My grandmother (on my father's and uncle's side) was a Temperance Christian of the old school who wouldn't allow publications like *Time* or *Life* into the house until she had scissored out the offensive beer and whiskey ads, which meant the articles often had important pieces missing. She kept a copy of Hal Lindsey's *The Late Great Planet Earth* in her bookcase along with other evangelical tomes, and when we visited her at her ancient Pittsburgh row house, the only secular reading material I could find to while away hot summer afternoons was a dusty anthology of poetry and short stories in which I first encountered Edgar Allan Poe's "The Raven." Her attic was crowded with fascinating relics: I remember early sound recordings on shellac disks, a battered Union Army rifle, and a primitive Zenith round-screen television that looked as if a cathedral radio had swallowed an oscilloscope. The time we spent with her during our annual pilgrimage from California to Pennsylvania must have been difficult for my parents, who were heavily addicted smokers but had to pretend they weren't, but for me, the only real inconvenience came at the dinner table when it was my turn to pronounce the communal blessing. I bowed my head and dutifully murmured the words, I hope not too obviously grudgingly.

When I was nine years old my father was offered a job in Toronto, and it was after we moved there that our church attendance became increasingly sporadic. We relocated within the city more than once, attending services at local churches of various denominations. The church I called Baptist in the first chapter of this book might have been a Methodist assembly or some other breed of low Protestant chapel—at the time I didn't much care, and I no longer remember. Many years later, applying for Canadian citizenship, when I had to dig out my parents' immigration records, I discovered they had put down their religious affiliation as "Disciples of Christ," to which my reaction was bewilderment. I wasn't sure I had ever heard of the denomination.

The upside to this theological cone of silence was that, because we never spoke about religious matters, I was never made to feel ashamed of my burgeoning atheism. Something I learned when I left home and made friends in the science fiction community is that others hadn't been so fortunate.

The science fiction subculture as I found it was intellectually diverse to the point of wholesale eccentricity, a Star Wars cantina of good and bad ideas. The editor of one of the major science fiction magazines until his death in 1971 was John W. Campbell, an ultraconservative who repeatedly promoted fringe notions, some more toxic than others. His hobbyhorses included General Semantics, parapsychology, and an alleged antigravity device called the Dean Drive. L. Ron Hubbard published his earliest version of Scientology, a pseudo-psychological theory he called Dianetics, in Campbell's magazine, where much of his science fiction writing had already appeared. (By "following the sharply defined basic laws dianetics sets forth," Campbell gushed in a cheerleading editorial, "physical ills such as ulcers, asthma and arthritis can be cured.")[3] At the same time, some of the field's most prominent writers were progressives and rationalists who took refuge in rival publications like *Galaxy* or *The Magazine of Fantasy and Science Fiction*. Join the bar crowd at any science fiction convention of the 1950s or '60s and you might overhear someone advocating for nudism, free love, Buddhism, or the psychic benefits of peyote. By the 1970s the science fiction writer Philip K. Dick had come to believe he was in telepathic contact with first-century Christians; his *Exegesis*, a nearly unreadable journal of freeform religious ideation, was eventually published as a thousand-page hardcover. In the circles of fandom I inhabited, atheism was probably the default setting, but I also mingled with Christians, Mormons (more usually ex-Mormons), secular Jews, observant Jews, Ayn Rand-worshipping Objectivists, and Timothy-Leary-style LSD enthusiasts. These categories sometimes commingled in unexpected ways. I have seen committed atheists earnestly casting the I Ching, for example.

But I also met people who might be thought of as refugees from religion, people whose experience of religion had been consistently and caustically negative. Some had been raised in suffocatingly strict Catholic or Protestant households. Some had endured personal conflicts with their families or their churches. Many, scientifically literate and intellectually curious, were aggrieved by attempts to curtail their curiosity or to discredit the biological or geological sciences. A growing number, as the 1970s advanced, were infuriated by attacks from an increasingly influential religious right on reproductive freedom, feminism, and the movement for LGBTQ equality.

The more thoughtful Christian apologists will acknowledge at least some of these problems but insist the responsibility can't be laid at the foot of religion in general or Christianity in particular. And there's a large kernel of truth in that. It's certainly true that there are Christian households and Christian churches that are neither oppressive nor unwelcoming. There are Christians who have no problem acknowledging scientific truths, and there have been Christians on the vanguard of the fight for LGBTQ rights and marriage equality. Still, *something* seems to connect all these grievances. Even if the offending parties can't and don't speak for Christianity as a whole or religion in general, they cloak themselves in religious doctrine, justify their behavior with Christian language, and speak with what they claim to be Christian authority. How should we evaluate that behavior?

* * *

"The legitimate powers of government," Thomas Jefferson said in *Notes on the State of Virginia*, "extend to such acts only as are injurious to others. But it does me no injury for my neighbour to say there are twenty gods, or no god. It neither picks my pocket nor breaks my leg."

Jefferson is making a call for tolerance here, and we need to honor it. But how do we do that when pockets have indeed been picked and legs have in fact been broken in the name of religion?

The first thing we should do is carve out some space for Christianity. Jefferson's maxim is truest when we apply it to purely metaphysical beliefs. Recall what the Christian philosopher Peter van Inwagen said: "there is no established body of metaphysical results." In metaphysics, "you are perfectly free to disagree with anything the acknowledged experts say." We can certainly *argue* with Christian metaphysics, and that argument is as old as Christian philosophy itself. But metaphysical claims can't be resolved the way disputes about the observable universe are routinely resolved. If someone tells me they believe reality is the creation of God, the most charitable thing I can do is to take that as an honest description of their state of mind. Their belief places no obligation on me, and unless I'm asked for my own opinion—which happens remarkably seldom—I don't need to contradict it. Atheists are not the Metaphysical Police. Christians are as entitled as anyone else to speculate about the nature of being.

But when a self-identified Christian insists, for instance, that the earth is only a few thousand years old, something has clearly gone haywire. We have an overwhelming preponderance of evidence that our planet is older than that by many orders of magnitude, and yet there are countless websites, blogs, books, podcasts, "museums," and theme parks dedicated to promoting Noachian flood scenarios, the supposed co-existence of human beings and dinosaurs, and similar absurdities. These fantasies are often presented to children as facts, or at least "alternative facts." There are well-funded and persistent political campaigns to force these notions to be taught in schools alongside of, or in place of, actual biological and geological science. In certain homeschooling or religious school environments, dissent from such ideas may be subtly or overtly punished. And in certain Christian communities, the rejection or denial of science is routinely valorized and contemporary science, or the teaching of it, is demonized and belittled.

What are these Christians doing wrong? The first instinct of atheists might be to say that creationists are ignoring or denying the evidence, and that certainly seems true. But we can also think of it this way: creationists are *overvaluing* Biblical evidence.

Stories from the Book of Genesis *are* evidence about the age of the earth, in the sense that they represent the historical beliefs of the community that created them. We know they are not *reliable* evidence about the age of the earth because they are flatly contradicted by the geological record. The question of the age of the earth is not materially different from, say, the question of whether a box of grocery-store doughnuts has passed its expiration date—in both cases, one consults the evidence at hand and draws a reasonable conclusion. Metaphysical beliefs, as such, have no bearing on the question. The solipsist, the theist, the pantheist, and the atheist can look at the same evidence and draw the same conclusion: these doughnuts passed their best-before date six months ago . . . whether there are twenty gods or no god.

Again, the problem is not that the creationist espouses a particular metaphysical belief. The problem is that the creationist is adducing his metaphysical belief as evidence. The creationist chain of reasoning might look something like this:

> *The Bible implies that the earth is approximately six thousand years old.*
>
> *The Bible is authoritative because it was inspired by the author of all reality.*
>
> *Any apparent physical evidence to the contrary is thus trivial by comparison.*
>
> *Therefore the earth is approximately six thousand years old.*

This is questionable at every step, but notice that the proposition "the Bible is inspired by the author of all reality" is a metaphysical claim (that such a being exists) paired with a historical claim (that such a being meaningfully influenced the composition of the Book of Genesis). Because these metaphysical claims are "not established," as Inwagen says, and because "you are perfectly free to disagree" with them, they *cannot* serve as evidence in a dispute about the age of an object such as the planet Earth or a box of doughnuts.

That doesn't mean that a scientist, or anyone else, is required to disregard or set aside his or her metaphysical convictions. A scientist who cherishes a belief that the universe was supernaturally created, like Fr. Georges Lemaître, might be inclined to ask questions that a scientist who holds a different belief would not, and that diversity of opinion can be a good thing—Lemaître was more right than wrong about the Big Bang. But while our diverse beliefs might contribute to forming a useful diversity of hypotheses, those beliefs can't simultaneously serve as evidence for those hypotheses. Georges Lemaître's Catholicism is not evidence that the Big Bang took place, and Lemaître knew this as well as anyone . . . which is perhaps why Pope Pius XII was reluctant to mention Lemaître by name even as he praised Lemaître's theory.

For the same reason, metaphysical beliefs are powerless to justify, excuse, or mandate acts of civil authority.

The history of Christianity is a long and complex one, and it would be simplistic to suggest that its history is one of unrelieved oppression, but it isn't hard to find examples of Christian institutions acting as instruments of oppression. Often the oppression we associate with Christianity has come at the hands of civil authorities rather than directly from the clergy or the magisterium, though the two are historically entangled and the church has usually served as an active enabler. For example, as I write this chapter, there are calls in Scotland to create a national memorial to the more than 2,500 women and men who were tortured and killed under the Witchcraft Act between 1563 and 1736. The Scottish king James VI (later James I of England), one of the driving forces behind the Act, was "notoriously obsessed with the malign influence of witches" and even composed his own book on the subject, *Daemonologie*—although, according to Edinburgh University historian Julian Goodare, the witch hunt "would have happened anyway because of the intensity of the Scottish Reformation" and the political influence of Church of Scotland parish elders.[4]

One famous victim of the Witchcraft Act was Agnes Sampson, accused of using witchcraft to raise storms that threatened the king as he sailed back from a visit to Denmark, a crime for which she was strangled and burned at the stake in 1591. Another was a woman named Lilias Adie, who died under torture in 1704 and was buried "on the shore at the village of Torryburn . . . under a hulking sandstone slab to prevent the devil from gaining access."[5] What the devil might have wanted with poor Lilias Adie's corpse was left unspoken. Others, however, apparently did have some use for it. Her skull was retrieved and put on public exhibit in the nineteenth century. A recent digital reconstruction of her face, based on photographs of that skull, shows an apparently gentle and unremarkable older woman utterly unlike the pop-culture representation of witches as crones and hags.

Lilias Adie's torture and death, and the Act that enabled it, was justified with metaphysical beliefs adduced as evidence; and the authority of those who pronounced against her, from the bench or from the pulpit, rested on a metaphysical gnosticism posing as unquestionable truth.

Obviously, brutal acts of oppression can be and have been justified in other ways. Countless dissidents have been tortured and executed in the name of ethnic purity, the dictatorship of the proletariat, the mandate of history, or at the whim of an authoritarian strongman. But too often throughout history, the metaphysical superstructure of religion has been deployed to excuse such oppression, and it continues to be cited in contemporary political debates. According to a speech at the Notre Dame Law School by former American Attorney General William Barr, social order can only follow from "commonly-shared moral values. And to control willful human beings, with an infinite capacity to rationalize, those moral values must rest on authority independent of men's will—they must flow from a transcendent Supreme Being."[6] (Or at least from someone claiming to speak on behalf of a "transcendent Supreme Being.") In a 2006 speech at the same venue, the current Supreme Court Justice Amy Coney Barrett recommended that graduates "keep in mind that your legal career is but a means to an end, and . . . that end is building the kingdom of God."[7] And these are only the most cautious, high-end expressions of a sentiment that, in its more reckless manifestations, is described as Christian Dominionism or Christian Nationalism. Frederick Clarkson described the three principles that unite the various strains of American Dominionism:

1. Dominionists celebrate Christian nationalism, in that they believe that the United States once was, and should once again be, a Christian nation. In this way, they deny the Enlightenment roots of American democracy.

2. Dominionists promote religious supremacy, insofar as they generally do not respect the equality of other religions, or even other versions of Christianity.

3. Dominionists endorse theocratic visions, insofar as they believe that the Ten Commandments, or "biblical law," should be the foundation of American law and that the U.S. Constitution should be seen as a vehicle for implementing Biblical principles.[8]

The risk is that anyone trying to oppose these ideas can be drawn into a fruitless metaphysical dispute. We need to keep in mind that the specific content of the metaphysical belief doesn't matter. Whether the claim emanates from a Supreme Court nominee, a Catholic bishop, a crazed Reddit post, or an irate Evangelical parent at a family dinner table, what is at stake is not the power or intention of God but the power and intention of the claimant. When Christians seek to restrict access to contraception, or to ban the teaching of biology in the public schools, it is their power to do so that needs to be called into question, not the particulars of their metaphysical beliefs.

It matters not whether my neighbor believes in twenty gods or no gods, as long as he isn't permitted to pick my pocket or break my leg.

* * *

Both my parents are deceased. I regret to say that I never had an adult conversation with either of them about religion or the relative absence of it in our household. But they were of the generation that had lived through the Depression and the Second World War, and I suspect their reticence about religion was not different from their similar discomfort with political or scientific talk. For them, as for many of their peers, religion and politics, and even science, were poisoned chalices from which had poured violent radicalism, a World War, a Cold War, a bristling nuclear arsenal, and all the other unsettling realities of mid-century America. That climate of opinion is sometimes described as conformity or anti-intellectualism, but it might be more charitable to think of it as the effort of Americans traumatized by war and economic insecurity to construct a safe, walled domesticity for themselves and their families.

It's difficult to reconstruct that mood today, but we can discern some of it from a few distinctive cultural artifacts. A 1952 film directed by Leo McCarey, *My Son John*, tells the story of an American family torn apart when the youngest of three sons comes home from college subtly changed. He refuses to attend church; he makes sardonic remarks about patriotism and football and the flag. Has John been corrupted by his teachers, perhaps to the point of espousing atheism—or even Communism? John, played with a sort of creepy effervescence by the late Robert Walker, is every conservative's nightmare, a left-wing cuckoo planted in a cozy American nest. *My Son John* may not be a horror movie, but it feels like a companion piece to another classic of 1950s American paranoia, *Invasion of the Body Snatchers*, and John himself is only one step away from the glow-eyed alien children in the British film *Village of the Damned*. *My Son John*, director Leo McCarey told the New York Times, is "about a mother and father who struggled and slaved. They had no education. They put all their money into higher education for their sons. But one of the kids gets too bright ... The mother knows only two books—her Bible and her cookbook. But who's brighter in the end—the mother or the son?"[9] In case the answer isn't obvious, it's the mother. Bookish, effete John is ultimately revealed as a Commie spy-in-training, gunned down in a taxi by his foreign masters when he repents and tries to turn himself in to the FBI. According to the *New Yorker*, the moral of the story is that "Americans ought to cut out thinking, obey their superiors blindly, regard all political suspects as guilty without tri-al, revel in joy through strength, and pay more attention to foot-ball."[10] But the film was vigorously promoted in other circles. The Catholic Institute of the Press adopted a resolution commending it. Senator Karl Mundt of South Dakota called it "the greatest and most stirring pro-American motion picture of the last decade."[11]

The movie is as uncomfortable to watch today as it must have been more than half a century ago, but it's a perfect exemplar of the kind of febrile anti-intellectualism that haunted many families in its time. Of course, all this cultural anxiety invited what Sig-mund Freud called "the return of the suppressed," a reaction that took the form of rock and roll, beat poetry, folk music, psychedel-ic drugs, avant-garde art, and, of course, science fiction. Some of my generation of postwar suburban children hid copies of Allen Ginsberg's *Howl* under their mattresses; some of us hid copies of Robert A. Heinlein's *Stranger in a Strange Land*. Many of us played out a real-life version of *My Son John* at university, or in the counterculture haunts of major cities, or at science fiction conven-tions. A few of us alarmed our families by trading in Christianity for atheism, Buddhism, or one of the quasi-cultic "human poten-tial" movements that were born in the fading echoes of the 1960s.

That dynamic may seem a little perplexing, seen from the fragmented cultural no-man's-land of 2021. We live in an age of different paranoias, confronting different threats. No single so-cial paradigm dominates the American media landscape the way Christian anticommunism could in the 1950s. Atheism is hardly universally accepted—a 2007 Gallup poll found that 53 percent of respondents would not vote for an otherwise qualified atheist in a presidential election—but atheists can at least raise their hands and speak up without risking an FBI interview. At the same time, the fear that a white, Christian national consensus is inexorably slipping away has helped fuel one of the most divisive and dan-gerous political moments in America since the 1850s. What in mid-twentieth-century America seemed like a defensive retreat from the world of ideas has turned into an all-out crusade against objective truth.

The culture wars are raging both inside and outside the church. A recent article by conservative commentator David Brooks lamented that "Evangelicalism has gone from the open evangelism of Billy Graham to the siege mentality of Franklin Graham."[12] At a moment of deep economic and political insecurity, perhaps Christians can be forgiven for retreating to structures that have traditionally provided an anchor point of moral stability and continuity, however illusory that might be. But for the crusading brand of Christian politics there is no such excuse. And there is nothing to be gained by deferring to the metaphysical beliefs of Dominionists, right-wing Evangelicals, or the theocratic wing of the Republican Party. The metaphysical gnosticism of these groups, however they may describe it, justifies nothing and excuses nothing. By insisting that God grants them unique authority over the rest of us, they plant one foot on a cloud and the other inside a prison.

* * *

The teapot bohemia I found in the science fiction subculture of the 1970s has since evolved into something more like the Japanese concept of *otaku*, a consuming interest in a particular hobby or niche cultural product, sometimes involving cosplay—a subculture, certainly, but not a counterculture in any meaningful sense. In a media landscape saturated with science fiction and fantasy, perhaps that's all it can be.

Of the friends and acquaintances I made through my involvement with science fiction, most have fared reasonably well. If our smorgasbord of metaphysical beliefs and non-beliefs hasn't lofted us to transcendence, at least it doesn't seem to have hurt us very much. Most of the atheists I knew in 1980 remain atheists, though some have grown more tentative in their convictions. We count among our numbers a few with successful careers in the publishing business, a few with university tenure, and a majority with lives not very different from other Americans of our generation.

But if the large question of the existence of God remains "not established," and if we are "perfectly free to disagree" with our Christian friends, does that mean we've arrived at an impasse?

Religious apologists will often insist that atheism, like theism, is a metaphysical belief. The choice is binary, they tell us. Either you believe reality is grounded in God, or you believe it isn't. Pick one. Or say the answer is unknowable, and call yourself agnostic.

Do those choices exhaust the possibilities? Perhaps not, if we're willing to ask the right questions.

6

Lost in Possibility Space

Is it *possible* that God exists?

The question is often asked of atheists. And atheists generally answer with a quick, qualified yes: *Well, sure, anything's possible.*
Often that answer is shorthand for an even more qualified answer:
Let's assume for the sake of argument that it's possible that God
exists, and get on with the discussion.

What comes next, if the theist who posed the question is well-
versed in Christian apologetics, is usually some version of what's
called the "ontological argument for the existence of God." The
ontological argument was first put forward by the twelfth-centu-
ry theologian Anselm of Canterbury, but its most-cited modern
descendant is probably the "modal" argument devised by Christian philosopher Alvin Plantinga. We don't need to look closely at
Plantinga's argument—it turns on a tricky definition of "necessary
existence"—except to note that one of its key premises (that "there
is a possible world in which maximal greatness is instantiated")
is yet another metaphysical assertion. As Plantinga himself ad-

mitted, while he thinks the premise is sound, "not everyone who understands and reflects on [it] will accept it."[1]

So is the initial question—"Is it possible that God exists?"—the wrong question?

Maybe not. In fact, it comes close to being the *right* question. As long as we don't answer it too hastily.

* * *

"Possibility" is a surprisingly slippery concept. It crops up in many different contexts. A philosopher might have one definition for it, a mathematician might have another. But all we need for our purposes is a colloquial definition. What do we mean when we say something is possible—or impossible?

Usually we call something "possible" if it doesn't defy our most elementary expectations about the way the world works. Is it possible that, tomorrow morning, I might wake up to find myself leading an army of sentient squirrels against an invasion of angry Martian robots? For all reasonable intents and purposes, no, that it is not possible. I am, of course, a science fiction writer, and I suppose I could construct a scenario in which such a thing *does* happen . . . but in order to do so at any level of plausibility I would have to address the obvious objections, including my own lack of military experience, the sparse supply of sentient squirrels, the difficulty of forming a squirrel-human alliance over the course of a single night, and the conspicuous absence of angry robots in our astronomical surveys of the surface of Mars. Colloquially, we would call such a scenario impossible. Since human beings are not granted absolute certainty with regard to future events, what we mean is that it seems extraordinarily unlikely. (To paraphrase the coroner of Munchkinland in the 1939 film version of *The Wizard of Oz*, it's not only merely unlikely, it's really most sincerely unlikely.) An enormous weight of evidence and prior experience argues against it.

To call something "possible," on the other hand, is to say that little or nothing in our prior experience appears to preclude it from existing or happening, even if it happens rarely. Asked in 1966 whether Bob Dylan would, in the twenty-first century, win a Nobel Prize for literature, an intelligent observer might scoff and say she doubted it, but "I guess it's not impossible"—meaning it doesn't seem like the sort of thing a panel of Nobel judges would do, but the Nobel Prize might be awarded differently in fifty years' time, or Dylan might by then have produced a genuinely Nobel-worthy body of work. Only one of those two things need be true to make the prediction plausible, and no fundamental assumption about reality or causality is violated if it turns out to be accurate.

Another way we use the word "possible" is to describe a situation from which many different outcomes might plausibly arise. We might say of Emily, a talented violinist who has just graduated from Julliard, that with regard to her career in music, "the possibilities are endless." Or perhaps a tech company has just devised a practical room-temperature superconductor, "opening up a whole new world of possibilities." Or maybe Eudena, along with her tribe of Paleolithic kinfolk, has discovered an unexplored river valley that offers fresh bounties of food and shelter, potentially transforming the lives of all involved: a place of tantalizing new possibilities. And so on. What's interesting here is that *unpredictability* has entered the conversation: many outcomes are apparently possible, and we don't know beforehand how events will play out. Biological evolution is an example of this kind of open-ended possibility. Even given a complete physical understanding of DNA, the future course of evolution is intrinsically unpredictable. The appearance of the first self-reproducing molecules on Earth began a causal chain that eventually produced penguins, pangolins, and piano players; but no extraterrestrial biologist, examining that first fleck of primordial life, could have *predicted* penguins, or pangolins, or piano players.

The concept of a *possibility space* is useful here. A possibility space is defined as some bounded condition in which various possible states can exist. The possibility space of a bottle filled with gaseous hydrogen, for instance, would be the sum of all the possible positions the molecules inside it could occupy. That's a long list, but it's a finite one. In his book *A World Beyond Physics*, Stuart A. Kaufman calls such lists "ergodic," meaning that "the system visits all its possible states" over some period of time: "The gas particles darting about in the bottle assume nearly every possible configuration before settling down into the stablest possible state." A "non-ergodic" possibility space, by contrast, is one in which there are too many possible states for the system to visit in a given time. Kaufman's example is the set of possible proteins of the length of two hundred amino acids:

> So if the 10 to the 80th particles in the universe were doing nothing since the Big Bang except making proteins in parallel at every tick of the Planck time clock, it would take 10 to the 39th power times the 13.7 billion year actual history of the universe to make all possible proteins of the length 200 amino acids, *just once*.[2]

The takeaway from this is that possibility spaces can be vast, perhaps unexplorably vast.

Because we're not mathematicians or physicists, we can use the concept of possibility space a little more loosely. The arts, for instance, tend to discover and occupy what we might call esthetic possibility spaces. The history of science fiction is an example. By the mid-nineteenth century it had become obvious that technological and scientific progress was transforming daily life in countless ways and would continue to do so. History, it seemed, was less like a predictable cycle of decay and resurrection, civilizations enjoying their day in the sun before weakening and yielding to a stronger new upstart, and more like a possibility space opened up by ongoing intellectual and technological progress, potentially alluring but also disturbingly unpredictable. This radical uncertainty about the future was part of what came to be called "modernity," and traditional literary forms and tropes struggled to address it. There were some notable efforts: Matthew Arnold's "Dover Beach," previously cited, for example, or Mary Shelley's *Frankenstein*, or Alfred Lord Tennyson's 1835 poem "Locksley Hall," in which the narrator muses about "the long result of Time" and the possibilities of the future:

> Men, my brothers, men the workers, ever reaping something
>   new:
> That which they have done but earnest of the things that they
>   shall do:
>
> For I dipt into the future, far as human eye could see,
> Saw the Vision of the world, and all the wonder that would be;
>
> Saw the heavens fill with commerce, argosies of magic sails,
> Pilots of the purple twilight dropping down with costly bales;
>
> Heard the heavens fill with shouting, and there rain'd a ghastly
>   dew
> From the nations' airy navies grappling in the central blue;
>
> Far along the world-wide whisper of the south-wind rushing
>   warm,
> With the standards of the peoples plunging thro' the thun-
>   der-storm;
>
> Till the war-drum throbb'd no longer, and the battle-flags were
>   furl'd
> In the Parliament of man, the Federation of the world.

As striking as these examples are, no distinct genre of literature arose from them. It was writers like Jules Verne and H. G. Wells, literalizing the future on the page, who opened the door into the possibility space of what came to be called science fiction. Their work fit awkwardly in the mainstream of literary tradition, but it would be eagerly adopted and imitated by the low-prestige popular fiction markets that thrived in early twentieth-century America.

Did Hugo Gernsback, who founded and edited the first pulp science fiction magazine *Amazing Stories* in 1926, realize he was exploring a new literary possibility space? He certainly would never have thought of it in those terms, but he may have sensed, at least, a public appetite for such stories and a potential profit to be extracted from them. His magazine initially reprinted stories by Wells and Verne and implicitly promised more of the same. That there could be "more of the same" implied a literary possibility space waiting to be explored. It was true that Wells in particular had not only opened the door into that space but had already plucked much of the low-hanging fruit. There are only a few familiar science-fictional ideas (space travel, time travel, futuristic utopias and dystopias) that aren't prefigured in some way by Wells's early novels and short stories. But much more remained to be said, and there were plenty of writers willing to say it.

And for the next century, that's what science fiction writers did. American pulp-magazine science fiction populated its possibility space with stories that seldom had much to boast about in terms of subtlety or finesse—this was a working-class literature, produced by women and men (predominantly men) who had in many cases learned their skills from other pulp writers and who conformed more or less willingly to the formulas and taboos of commercial fiction—but the ongoing technological transformation of every area of life from courtship to warfare gave them an enormous palette to work with. Stories about exploring the solar system raised the question of exploring other stars; stories about colonizing the galaxy raised the question of how such wide-flung civilizations could be organized or governed; and the many possible answers to that question gave us a small library of notable novels and stories including Isaac Asimov's *Foundation* trilogy, Frank Herbert's *Dune*, Samuel Delany's *Nova*, and contemporary work like Iain M. Banks's Culture series and Ann Leckie's *Ancillary Justice*. In the same way, *War of the Worlds*, the H. G. Wells novel that contemplated the prospect of an extraterrestrial invasion of Earth, can count among its mutant descendants Jack Finney's *Invasion of the Body Snatchers*, Arthur C. Clarke's *Childhood's End*, and my own novel *Spin*. And so on.

Any artistic possibility space can be quickly populated, or overpopulated, and its supply of novelty may decline as its tropes become increasingly generic. To some degree that may have happened with science fiction, as it has with the once-dominant Western genre. But science fiction has the advantage of exploring a constantly evolving external possibility space: the very real possibilities opened up by ongoing waves of technological, cultural, and scientific change. Postwar American science fiction writers peered into a future defined by what they had experienced of that change, and the prospects they imagined could be horrifying (nuclear war envisioned as an end to civilization, or at least an interregnum between our civilization and whatever might rise from its radioactive ashes) or edifying (a scenario of unlimited technological progress that would hand over tedious work to robots and ultimately carry us to the stars). Serious science fiction writers working in the year 2021 confront a rather different external possibility space, one defined by ecological crises, global conflict, artificial intelligence, digital surveillance, and a host of potentially invasive new mind/body technologies. Some traditional tropes, such as interstellar travel, have increasingly been handed off to the fantasy genre. As early as 1977, George Lucas's original *Star Wars* movie placed its interstellar narrative not in the future but in a mythical past, in an ontology more Gandalfian than Einsteinian. One recent novel about star travel, Kim Stanley Robinson's *Aurora*, makes the case that interstellar colonization will always be a quixotic and impractical project. But all is not necessarily doom and gloom. An even more recent novel by Robinson, *The Ministry for the Future*, meticulously imagines a process by which humanity might overcome the current climate crisis. The recent (sadly belated) opening of the genre to non-white, non-male, non-gender-conforming voices has created new entryways to fresh possibility spaces. For all the problems we're confronting as a species, the future remains wide open to imaginative exploration.

* * *

We've teased out a couple of ways of thinking about possibility (and impossibility), so let's pin these down more formally. For the purpose of answering the question posed at the beginning of this chapter, we can talk about these in terms of *impossibility*.

One kind of impossibility is what we might call ontological impossibility, or impossibility in principle. For some defined framework—let's say, the observable universe—there may be events or phenomena that simply cannot exist. It may be the case, for instance, that in our universe a large object such as a planet cannot possess mass and momentum and yet remain unaffected by gravity. I would be willing to bet that's true ... but since I don't entirely understand the physics of gravitation, and since I don't have any comprehensive knowledge about how exceptions might occur, and since I know our understanding of matter and energy remains incomplete, I have to hedge my bet and call it extraordinarily unlikely. Nevertheless, it may truly be the case that such an object simply cannot exist. Some imaginable phenomena may in fact be categorically impossible.

A subset of ontological impossibility is *logical impossibility*, in which a proposition can be called impossible if it contradicts itself ("a square circle") or if it violates some stated set of fundamental rules (e.g., for simple decimal arithmetic, it is impossible that 2 plus 2 equals 5). But even logical impossibility needs to be qualified once we begin to apply it to the real world. The apparent logical impossibility of an object being in two places at once, for instance, is in some arguable sense violated in the experimental results that arise from quantum phenomena. This doesn't prove that logic is somehow meaningless—logic, after all, is what helps us draw inferences from observation, even in quantum physics—but it does illustrate the fact that there are realms where our *intuitions* about what's logically impossible begin to fail us. So we're forced to hedge even that apparently sure-thing bet. And what does a bet on ontological impossibility look like, once we've hedged it?

It looks, once again, like *extreme unlikeliness*, following from an observer's prior experience and available evidence. We can call this state of affairs *provisional* impossibility, or *likely* impossibility. The concept of possibility and impossibility will always be hedged, from any given observer's point of view, by the limitations of the observer's knowledge and experience.

The third useful idea we've developed is the concept of possibility space, using the word "space" to talk about any bounded realm containing a set of unknown objects, phenomena, or potential outcomes. Hence we can talk about a musical possibility space, like jazz; a literary possibility space, like science fiction; a physical possibility space, like the set of all possible proteins containing two hundred amino acids; or a biological possibility space, like the set of all living things that could be produced by the mechanism of evolution.

Given all that, let's look back at the original question. Is it possible that God exists?

* * *

God is defined in the Christian philosophical tradition as a metaphysical being, an uncaused cause at the root of all reality. The question, once we unpack it, is whether it's possible that metaphysical reality actually conforms to the theistic description of it. But notice something interesting: the set of all potential descriptions of metaphysical reality is a *possibility space*.

Christian theism is just one of many proposed descriptions of metaphysical reality. Other faiths offer different descriptions—metaphysical realities governed by a different God, or by dual gods, or by multiple gods; metaphysical realities involving epicycles of creation and destruction, or metaphysical realities with fixed teleological destinations; finite and infinite metaphysical realities, and so on. And, of course, potential descriptions of metaphysical reality need not invoke deities at all. Non-theistic descriptions of metaphysical reality might include, for instance, physicist Max Tegmark's proposal that "mathematical existence equals physical existence" and that "all structures that exist mathematically exist physically as well."[3] Tegmark calls this a "Level IV multiverse," but since the subtitle of his book is "My Quest for the Ultimate Nature of Reality," we can safely say it meets our definition of a metaphysical claim.

There are only two constraints on potential descriptions of ultimate reality: they must be self-consistent, and they must be compatible with the fact of personal experience. Any self-contradictory or incoherent description of ultimate reality can probably be ruled out—though we have to be careful about what we call logically impossible, in light of our chastening experience with quantum physics—as can any description that somehow precludes our own lived experience of the world, given that we do in fact experience it. But those boundaries are extraordinarily generous. How many potential descriptions of ultimate reality might exist within those limits? They would have to include:

- All theistic descriptions, past and present;

- Any conceivable theistic description not yet proposed;

- All non-theistic descriptions, past and present;

- Any conceivable non-theistic description not yet proposed;

- All potential descriptions of metaphysical reality that are knowable in principle;

- All potential descriptions of metaphysical reality that are unknowable in principle, and so on.

Some descriptions of metaphysical reality may entail an unknown number of spatial dimensions, or an unknown number of temporal dimensions, or an unknown number of dimensions that are neither temporal nor spatial, whatever that might mean. Some may describe metaphysical realities that are finite or unbounded in any or all of these dimensions. A true description of metaphysical reality might defy our ability to understand it—the number of potentially true descriptions of metaphysical reality might be larger than the subset of descriptions that can be comprehended by a finite human mind.

That's a big possibility space! It may, in fact, be an infinitely large possibility space. We have no way of knowing whether the list of all possible descriptions of metaphysical reality is finite or countable. And any particular description of metaphysical reality, despite being coherent and consistent with our experience, might be *categorically* impossible if some other such description turns out to be the true one.

Keep that last point in mind. Is it possible that God exists? We have to resist the temptation to say yes, because the true description of metaphysical reality might rule out the existence of such a being. We cannot say with certainty that it's impossible that God exists, but we *can* say with certainty that it *might* be impossible that God exists. So let me answer the question for myself, as honestly and carefully as I can, given the limits of my knowledge and the vastness of metaphysical possibility space:

I *don't know* whether it's possible that God exists. (Do you?)

* * *

But isn't that just agnosticism? Have we traveled all this way just to arrive at a wishy-washy gosh-I-don't-know conclusion about the existence of God?

No. This is not an agnosticism that treats the existence of God as a coin toss, heads God exists, tails God doesn't. This is not, in fact, an agnosticism about God at all. This is a generalized metaphysical agnosticism, arising from a careful inventory of personal knowledge. It's an admission that I don't know which of countlessly many potential descriptions of ultimate reality might be the true one. And, perhaps surprisingly, that admission doesn't preclude a robust personal atheism. In fact, it bolsters it, as we'll see in the next chapter.

7

Asking a Better Question

The English town of Tunbridge Wells, in the latter half of the eighteenth century, was a tourist destination located about thirty-six miles from London. "The town itself is but indifferent," *London Magazine* wrote in 1749, "and the streets ill-paved; but what renders it famous, is the medicinal wells ... which occasion an annual resort of abundance of people of fashion, some for health, but more for diversion."[1]

In other words, the town was a popular summer destination for the horse-and-buggy equivalent of the jet set. One of those fashionable habitués was a woman named Elizabeth Montague, who wrote to a friend that "Tunbridge seems the very parliament of the world, where every country and every rank has its representatives," including visitors from Hungary, Italy, France, and Portugal. In another letter she was less enthusiastic: "I never saw a worse collection of human creatures in all my life. My comfort is, that as there are not many of them I ever saw before, I flatter myself that there are few of them I shall ever see again."[2]

No one has recorded what the permanent residents of Tunbridge Wells felt about this annual influx of the European *beau monde*, but they probably reacted with the same mixture of love and loathing the occupants of modern-day resorts like Bar Harbor bring to the "summer people" who clog their streets and keep the cash registers ringing between Memorial Day and Labor Day. One such resident, who would have trodden the unpaved streets of Tunbridge Wells even in the muddy off-season, was another of our clergyman-scientists, a mathematician and Presbyterian minister named Thomas Bayes. Bayes came from a Nonconformist family in Sheffield, "Nonconformist" referring to a long-standing dispute over whether the Church of England should be required by law to use the *Book of Common Prayer* in its services. As trivial as this controversy might sound to modern ears, in the seventeenth and early eighteenth centuries it was hotly debated both in the pulpit and in Parliament. The *Book of Common Prayer* had been composed by Thomas Cranmer in 1549; in 1553 Cranmer was burned at the stake for heresy and the book removed from circulation; in 1559, under Elizabeth I, Parliament passed an Act of Uniformity that required all churches to use Cranmer's book … and so it went, with the book being once again proscribed during the Commonwealth period and made mandatory again with a second Act of Uniformity in 1660. Versions of it are still in use today, and there are well-known English phrases that derive from it: "Ashes to ashes, dust to dust;" "In the midst of life, we are in death."

The universities of Oxford and Cambridge were closed to Nonconformists, who refused to defer to the law requiring the use of the *Book of Common Prayer*, which led Bayes to study for the Presbyterian ministry at the more tolerant University of Edinburgh. After a stint in London, he settled in Tunbridge Wells sometime around 1734. Whether he ever enjoyed the famous medicinal baths remains unknown. His first publication was a theological work (*Divine Benevolence: or, An Attempt to Prove that the Principal End of the Divine Providence and Government is the Hap-*

piness of His Creatures), but he is better remembered for his work in the mathematics of statistics and probability.

Let me immediately allay any fear that we're about to jump into a discussion of mathematical probability. It's not my field, and I'm hardly equipped to explain it even to myself. But since Bayes' Theorem has become a staple of discourse around atheism, it might help to understand the basics of what it is and what some of its applications are.

The equation for Bayes' Theorem can be written in various ways depending on the data you want to analyze, but for our purposes we can write it this way:

$$P(B|E) = \frac{P(B)\,P(E|B)}{P(E)}$$

—which looks intimidating, but the terms are fairly easy to understand. **P** is probability, **B** is a belief, and **E** is evidence.

The theorem has applications across the sciences—really, anywhere statistical analysis and probabilities are important—ranging from economics to neuroscience to machine learning and artificial intelligence. Atheists and theists have deployed it in arguments and counter-arguments about the existence of God, the historicity of the Gospels, and the plausibility of the Resurrection. But, without delving into the math, what does it mean? "The most dumbed-down description," according to John Horgan at *Scientific American*, is, "Initial belief plus new evidence = new and improved belief."

Or, "the fuller version," which I'll paraphrase from Horgan and divide into four parts for clarity:

- The probability that a belief is true, in light of new evidence, equals
- the probability that the belief is true *regardless* of that evidence,
- multiplied by the probability that the evidence is true *given that the belief is true*,

- divided by the probability that the evidence is true *regardless* of whether the belief is true.[3]

Lost yet? No matter. What's important is that Thomas Bayes, from his ministry at the dour Presbyterian Mount Sion Chapel in the eighteenth-century tourist resort of Tunbridge Wells, discovered a way to formally describe the process by which we estimate probabilities and revise those probabilities in light of fresh information. This is something we all do—when we step outside and try to guess whether it's likely to rain, for instance—though we don't consciously calculate the odds according to Bayes' Theorem any more than a baseball pitcher consciously calculates the Newtonian dynamics of a ball thrown at a given speed in a given direction. A certain kind of Bayesianism is built into our basic intuitions about what's plausible and what's not. It's an imperfect, approximate Bayesianism, subject to all our cognitive deficits and subjective errors, but it's good enough to help us get through the day without walking off a cliff or stepping in front of traffic.

Of course, the system works best when we're honest about what we know—and what we don't.

* * *

I've described the science fiction community I found in the 1970s as a "teacup bohemia," and it was certainly that. But it was something else, too, something more disconcerting for the person I was at twenty years old.

I had been a bookish kid, a constant reader, but not an especially talented student. In high school I excelled in a couple of subjects and barely scraped by in the rest. Nothing about my scholastic record would have impressed the office of admissions at any reputable university, but that didn't matter, because I wasn't bound for university. Neither of my older siblings had received any kind of post-secondary education, nor had my mother or my father.

We were not a wealthy family, although my father had done well enough in the booming postwar economy, moving to Los Angeles from Pittsburgh to work as a salesman for a greeting card company and eventually being offered an executive position at a Toronto branch plant. (He took me to work with him once or twice, to a brick building in Toronto's Leaside district. The huge, loud printing presses on the factory floor fascinated me; the managerial and editorial offices, reeking of cigarette smoke and connected by dim corridors painted a sickly shade of green, did not.)

Despite a conspicuously mediocre academic record, in my high-school crowd I had been the go-to guy for obscure information and science trivia. I was not athletic (far from it), and I was burdened with a nearly pathological shyness, but I was already obsessed with writing fiction, and I could turn out a decent paragraph—the ability to put together a coherent and grammatical essay balanced my inability to pay attention to any subject that didn't immediately interest me. That is to say, I managed to slide through high school by exercising a gift for language and a certain modicum of native intelligence. Some days, it felt like a kind of superpower—a lonely and diffident kid's way to evade attention and navigate a terrifying social landscape.

But I didn't finish high school. My father, a chain smoker, was diagnosed with lung cancer the year I turned eighteen, and I left school to help my mother take care of him as his health declined. After his death, when my mother moved back to California, I struck out on my own in Toronto. It was a time when anyone with decent keyboard skills could land a clerical job with the Ontario government, which I did, and for support I leaned on the community of science fiction enthusiasts and aspiring writers I had lately joined.

But that community wasn't just intellectually diverse, it was populated with more than its share of polymaths, graduate students, and obsessive autodidacts, few of whom were impressed by either my general knowledge or my gift for composing a readable sentence. At the age of nineteen I had already managed to sell a short story to a major science fiction market—under the byline "Bob Chuck Wilson," which endlessly amused my friends but was intended as an homage to my father, Charles Wilson, who had been known as Chuck. But it would be another ten years before I managed to place another work of fiction, and whatever cachet I gained from that single early sale evaporated fairly quickly.

In other words, a lonely and socially insular know-it-all had more than met his match. My superpower didn't work anymore. Whether the subject was literature, politics, history, science, anything from the geology of Canada to the poetry of Catullus, I was routinely outgunned and frequently embarrassed by my own naïveté. And like many painful but non-lethal experiences, this one eventually taught me some useful lessons.

The first and most important lesson was not to pretend to knowledge I didn't possess. I would like to say this conviction arose from moral principles, but it was really only acknowledging the obvious. I was a bad liar, and being caught at it was more humiliating than admitting ignorance. Better to keep my mouth shut and possibly learn a thing or two, even at the expense of my own vanity.

A second lesson, more difficult to learn, was that I shouldn't try to compensate for my own confusion by uncritically adopting other people's intellectual or ethical certainties. In those days, whenever I ventured to express doubt, there was always someone nearby who was more than happy to set me straight—according to their lights, and often with a degree of self-righteousness that rivaled anything I had encountered in the religion of my childhood. That kind of confidence can be deeply attractive to an insecure twenty-year-old who longs to borrow it as a shield against, or a disguise for, his own shortcomings. But in the end it amounted to nothing more than a roundabout way of making claims I wasn't in a position to honestly defend.

The world has a way of sanding down such moral splinters, except when it doesn't. The science fiction genre has produced a few notorious poseurs, the most conspicuous example being L. Ron Hubbard, who leveraged his success as a 1940s pulp writer into a far more lucrative and infinitely more destructive career as the head of a pseudo-scientific pop-psychology project (Dianetics) that subsequently evolved into a pseudo-religious business empire (Scientology) with a global reach. (Attempts by Scientologists to bloc-vote a Hugo Award for later Hubbard science fiction novels like *Black Genesis* or the ponderous *Battlefield Earth* failed decisively. *Black Genesis* made the final ballot in 1983 but placed behind "No Award.") Even writers vastly more talented than Hubbard, such as Robert A. Heinlein, have occasionally succumbed to the temptation to pronounce ex-cathedra on moral, metaphysical, and political matters. Heinlein's 1961 novel *Stranger in a Strange Land*, about an orphan raised by Martians who founds a new religion back on Earth, became a college-campus hit around the same time Timothy Leary was advising his followers to "start your own religion," and the book garnered Heinlein a certain countercultural cachet at a time when his political views were shifting decisively to the right. To his credit, Heinlein didn't accept the hippie-guru mantle that was offered to him, but his fiction did take on an increasingly blunt didactic tone in the late sixties and seventies. His 1973 novel *Time Enough for Love*, for instance, features page after page of aphorisms "from the notebooks of Lazarus Long," including items like "The greatest productive force is human selfishness" and "A man does not insist on physical beauty in a woman who builds up his morale." In the string of excellent young-adult novels he published in the 1950s (*Red Planet* and *Tunnel in the Sky*, among many others), Heinlein's protagonists were often conflicted and unsure of themselves, but by the late sixties that nod toward epistemic modesty had all but vanished from his work.

The lesson is not that writers should shun politics, or that writers should not be opinionated. The lesson is that writers of fiction are best served by an honest appraisal of their own state of knowledge. Fiction exists on the boundary between knowledge and invention, and a writer should have at least a vague notion of where that boundary is situated . . . perhaps especially science fiction writers, who often sidestep an established fact (the relativistic limits on interstellar travel, say) to explore larger truths about the world we live in.

But complete honesty is, of course, a chimera. We deceive ourselves as often and as easily as we deceive others, and the border between reason and rationalization can be hard to map. The branch of philosophy that deals with knowledge is called epistemology, and, unsurprisingly, theology has left many footprints there. Contemporary Christian philosopher Alvin Plantinga famously advocates for a model called "reformed epistemology," which borrows from John Calvin the idea of an innate human experience of the existence of God. In Plantinga's view, belief in God is "properly basic"—rational and warranted, even in the absence of evidence or argument. If your mind and body are working properly, Plantinga claims, knowledge of God follows as naturally as the knowledge that you possess fingers and toes. This is plausible, however, only to the degree that Plantinga's argument is plausible, and it seems like a thin reed to cling to, given that we have plenty of evidence—"Bayesian priors," in probability-speak—that distinguished philosophers of religion are not infallible and that finely-tuned philosophical arguments are not perfectly reliable guides to truth.

Knowledge is slippery. Even in matters that can be decided evidentially, as Reverend Bayes reminds us from his pulpit at Tunbridge Wells, the best we can hope for is a preponderance of evidence and, consequently, a high degree of probability—never "certainty." It's often easier to speak confidently about what we *don't* know than about what we do.

* * *

Let's imagine we're having a drink, you and I—say, in the bar at a Four Seasons hotel in Florida where a science fiction convention is underway—and we're accosted by a stranger—call him Frank—who in the course of conversation makes a strikingly unusual claim. There is, Frank insists, an inhabited planet in our galaxy ruled by a slug-shaped monarch named Trebor, who wears a crown of luminous vines and armor made of recycled spaceship parts.

Is the claim true? Most of us would say no, *of course* it's not true. But where does our confidence come from?

Another obvious (and honest) answer is that we *don't know* whether it's true. We don't have an interstellar guidebook to consult, after all. We can't say for sure what might be happening on worlds as yet undiscovered by Earthlings. But we can break down the claim a little more systematically, using some tools we've purloined from Reverend Bayes. And on closer inspection, it turns out that Frank's statement isn't a single claim but an amalgam of different claims. So let's divide it into its component parts and inspect them one at a time:

1. There are other habitable planets in our galaxy.

Are there? *I don't know*, but astronomers estimate that there are between 100 billion and 400 billion stars in the Milky Way. We can assume that many or most of them play host to planets of one kind or another, and it's far from impossible that some or many of these planets are warm enough, wet enough, old enough, and stable enough to support recognizable living ecologies. So let's be generous and say it's *very likely* that our galaxy harbors a large number of habitable planets. Score that point for Frank, then, but let's keep going.

2. Some of these planets currently host intelligent life.

Do they? *I don't know*, but it took at least 3.5 billion years for life on Earth to produce the kind of complex animals we might plausibly call intelligent. The implication is that planets with intelligent life will probably be a tiny fraction of the set of planets that are biologically active. So whatever the odds we give on whether proposition 1 is true, it's vastly *less* likely that 2 is true. (This causes Frank to frown.)

3. **At least one such planet currently hosts a civilization similar to ours.**

Does it? *I don't know*, but what we're calling "civilization" has existed on Earth for only an infinitesimal fraction of the time human beings have existed, so this pushes the cumulative odds lower still.

4. **The intelligent inhabitants of this planet are slug-shaped.**

Are they? *I don't know*, but evolution on Earth has produced a great variety of physical shapes—"endless forms most beautiful and wonderful," as Charles Darwin put it—and there's no reason to assume that different worlds with different evolutionary histories would be any less fecund. In other words, the possibility space for the shapes of differently evolved intelligent beings is immensely large. And in a case where we don't know which possibility is more likely, we have to assign equal probability to each possibility, including "creatures shaped like slugs." Which takes the cumulative likelihood down another big notch, and at this point, Frank is beginning to clench his fists and give us some serious side-eye.

5. **The extraterrestrial civilization in question is ruled by a monarchy.**

Is it? *I don't know*, but "monarchy" is surely a small fraction of "all possible systems of governance by which an alien civilization might be ruled." And now the cumulative likelihood of Frank's claim is beginning to look small enough that we'll need a decimal point and a big bag of zeroes to describe it.

6. The reigning monarch of this planet is named Trebor.

Is it? *I don't know*, but the set of names that might be given to an alien monarch is another vastly large possibility space, so we can understand why Frank has begun muttering into the drink the bartender put in front of him.

At this point nothing remains of Frank's original claim but Trebor's crown of luminous vines and his armor made of spaceship parts, and while those are lovely details, they add yet another truckload of zeroes after the decimal point.

All those *I-don't-knows* are additive. It might be reasonable to describe ourselves as agnostic about the existence of habitable planets in the galaxy, but when it comes to Trebor and his fashion accessories we've arrived at something nearly indistinguishable from outright disbelief. Does Trebor exist? Almost certainly not. Our conclusion is that it is *extraordinarily unlikely* that Frank's claim is true.

"Seems like nothing would convince you cynical bastards," Frank says, but he's mistaken about that. Reverend Bayes reminds us that there might be evidence for Frank's proposition we haven't yet considered, evidence that would turn the odds in a completely different direction. So we ask Frank where he got his idea about Trebor's planet.

"From myself," Frank says. "It's my idea. Straight from the horse's mouth."

Okay. But that amounts to a different claim, that Frank is a reliable source of knowledge about life on other planets. "How did you arrive at it?"

"It came to me in a dream."

We believe him. But we have plenty of evidence—Bayesian priors—that "it came to me in a dream" is not a guarantor of reliability. "It came to me in a dream" is likely to be true even if the claim itself is false. The numbers haven't budged.

Frank finishes his drink and stands up. Turns out he's a *South Park* fan, and he gives us his best Eric Cartman impression—"Screw you guys!"—as he stalks away.

* * *

The point here is not to construct an absurd caricature of theism or of Christianity in order to ridicule it. The point is to use a ridiculous example to show why our initial skepticism about Frank's claim is fully justified, even when we don't have direct knowledge about what happens on other inhabited planets in the galaxy.

Consider how *different* Frank's claim is from the claims of Christian theism. The broadest and most general component of Frank's claim is that "there are other habitable planets in our galaxy." As sweeping as that statement is, we can evaluate it with plenty of prior evidence in hand. We know what a galaxy is; we have an accumulation of scientific analyses of galaxies both near and far; we know what stars are; we know how stars vary in size and age; we know where, in principle, the habitable zones of various stars are located; we know that a great many stars harbor planets; we know that some of the exoplanets we have discovered occupy that habitable zone; we know that life evolved over a great span of time on our world and might have similarly evolved on other worlds—and so on.

The most sweeping claim we can extract from classical theism is a much broader one: *Reality at all times and all places was created by an uncaused metaphysical being.* And for that proposition we don't have anything like the kind of Bayesian priors we have for Frank's claim about inhabited worlds in the Milky Way galaxy. Is the theistic proposition true? *I don't know*: in the words of the nineteenth-century American agnostic Robert Ingersoll, "I do not pretend to tell what all the truth is. I do not pretend to have fathomed the abyss, nor to have floated on outstretched wings level with the dim heights of thought."[4]

Which is precisely why "Does God exist?" is the wrong question. It requires us to definitively answer a question philosophers have wrangled with for centuries without producing, as von Inwagen says, "a result." The debate is eternally interesting, but the debate is also eternally inconclusive.

Is there a better question?

Christian apologists will sometimes pose a more interesting one: is belief in God rational? Which takes us closer to something we can meaningfully engage, but falls short because it wants a single, categorical, binary response: is belief in God rational *in principle*, or is it not? And that requirement pushes us back into the glades of epistemic speculation, trying to answer the question not just for ourselves but for every conceivable person.

But what we really want is a personal answer, which implies a subtly different question:

Is it reasonable for me, situated as I am and with the knowledge I possess, to believe that God exists?

As we've seen, theism generally and Christianity in particular are forms of metaphysical gnosticism. To assert that God exists is to assert knowledge about all of reality at all times and all places. So let's begin to answer our question by asking an even more fundamental one about ourselves:

Do I possess reliable knowledge about metaphysical reality?

The answer—for me, from where I stand—is an easy *no*. The most reliable knowledge I can claim to possess falls within the boundary of the distant past, the foreseeable future, the very small, and the very large. I can say with something approaching certainty that *I do not possess reliable knowledge about metaphysical reality*. In other words, *It would be unreasonable for me to claim reliable knowledge about the nature of metaphysical reality.*

We can describe that answer as *personal metaphysical agnosticism*. But is there anything more specific we can say about belief in God? Can we get from a general metaphysical agnosticism to something that could plausibly be called atheism?

We've noted before that the set of potential descriptions of metaphysical reality comprises an enormously large possibility space. If we suppose a comprehensive description of metaphysical reality is even possible—and that's not a foregone conclusion—classical theism would still be just one among countless other descriptions. Think of any such description as a grain of sand buried among other grains on an incalculably large, cosmically large, perhaps even infinitely large beach. Individuals and communities of faith throughout recorded history have advanced many models of metaphysical reality, but what are the odds that any single such description is the correct one? If we assign equal probability to every possible description, the likelihood is almost infinitesimally small.

And "God exists," as we've seen, isn't a simple proposition. Any theological description of God has to be particularized, if for no other reason than to distinguish it from competing descriptions of a God or gods. But what we learned from our interaction with Frank is that adding detail to a largely unknown generality only introduces new levels of uncertainty. Breaking it down in the same way, from the most general claim to the most specific:

1. **There is a single true and comprehensible description of metaphysical reality.**

Is there? *I don't know*—I'm in no position to evaluate the absolute limits on truth and comprehensibility—and, to be honest, I have no idea how you would even begin to assign a probability to that claim. But we can be generous for the purposes of discussion and call it fifty/fifty.

2. **Reality at all times and all places was created by an uncaused metaphysical being.**

Was it? *I don't know*, but since I have no way of determining whether this is more or less probably true than any other possible description of the causal structure of metaphysical reality, I'm forced to assign it a correspondingly low likelihood.

3. **That being is omniscient, omnipresent, and maximally benevolent.**

Is it? *I don't know*, but it doesn't necessarily follow from (2), so we've lowered the cumulative likelihood another few orders of magnitude.

4. **That being is interested in the thoughts and behavior of human beings.**

You can see where this is going.

5. **That being is capable of sustaining human life after death.**

And so on, including *That being inspired the writing of the New and Old Testaments* and *That being entered into a covenant with the tribes of Israel* and *That being created a divine/human entity who lived in Judea in the First Century* and *That being caused Jesus to rise from the dead*. My metaphysical agnosticism makes it impossible for me to proclaim the existence of God, but the particularized description of God in classical theology means that—from where I stand—the claim that such a being exists looks *extraordinarily unlikely to be true*.

And since "extraordinarily likely" or "extraordinarily unlikely" is as close as we mortals can get to certainty, that conclusion is, in the end, indistinguishable from atheism.

8

Objections: A Dialogue

"I have a few objections to what you've written..."

"Wait, who are you?"

"I'm your imaginary Christian interlocutor. I'm here to raise some important questions you haven't addressed."

"Ah. Okay. Well, pull up a chair. Can I get you something to drink?"

"Seeing as how I'm imaginary, no. Nor will the chair be necessary. Although you're free to imagine one."

"I guess that simplifies things. Can I imagine a name for you?"

"If you like. Preferably not 'Frank'."

"How about Chris?"

"Cute. Fine. Shall we begin?"

"Fire away."

* * *

1. Is this version of atheism actually conciliatory?

Chris pulls up his imaginary chair. Snow is falling outside the window of my home office, the afternoon has begun its long subsidence into evening, and the room is a cozy citadel against a deepening winter. It feels like a good time to speak quietly about the large things of the world.

"In this book," Chris begins, "you repeatedly say you're speaking for yourself, describing your own personal state of knowledge."

"Well, yes. That's a key point. I'm in no position to make sweeping truth claims about ultimate reality, and my atheism follows from that fact."

"*Your* atheism. But isn't that a little disingenuous? The obvious implication is that others are in a similar position. If it's irrational for you to proclaim the existence of God, it's probably irrational for the rest of us."

"Maybe. You can draw your own conclusions, as I encourage readers to do. But I'm not trying to police other people's cherished metaphysical beliefs—and how could I, even if I wanted to? No conflict arises between us unless you insist that I acknowledge your beliefs as true, or that I accept them as evidence, or that I govern my behavior by them."

"Mmm ... that's easy to say, and it *sounds* conciliatory. But Christianity is an evangelical faith. Asking people to share our beliefs is what we do."

"Which is one reason why I'm not a Christian."

"Clearly! You've gone to great lengths to justify your identity as an atheist—"

"Hang on. Atheism isn't my 'identity.' My atheism is an entailment of my metaphysical agnosticism, and my metaphysical agnosticism, again, is just an inventory of my state of knowledge."

"But you're using it to draw lines in the sand. You would bar Christians from making law, for instance, and all because of—what did you call it? An inventory of your personal state of knowledge?"

"Let me be explicit, in case others make the same mistake you're making. I'm not advocating that Christians be 'barred' from anything at all. You're fully entitled to whatever beliefs about ultimate reality you may have, and you're fully entitled to participate in democratic politics. But, again, no one is reasonably obliged to acknowledge your metaphysical beliefs as true. No one is obliged to accept your metaphysical beliefs as evidence, in disputes that can be resolved evidentially. And no one is obliged to govern his behavior in accordance with your metaphysical beliefs."

"What you're describing is just secularism."

"You're welcome to call it that."

"And it leaves no room for the religious person in the public square."

"On the contrary. It leaves room for *every* religious person in the public square. If your participation is motivated in some part by your metaphysical convictions, that's fine. Conduct yourself accordingly. No one is stopping you."

"No? The moment a Christian expresses opposition to, say, same-sex marriage, he's condemned from all sides."

"You mean, the way homosexuals were once condemned from all sides? But that was different, wasn't it? Historically, LGBTQ people weren't just condemned. They were shamed. They were ostracized. They were criminalized. Sometimes they were imprisoned or subjected to 'cures' that amounted to torture. Sometimes they still are."

"Sure, and maybe those laws were wrong, in hindsight—but you would prevent us from writing *any* laws that acknowledge the sinful nature of homosexuality."

"I can't prevent you from trying to write laws. You can argue all you want for any law you care to propose. But you can't rationally expect others to endorse that legislation just because it accords with your particular metaphysical beliefs."

"But that principle has the effect of exiling Christians from the public square. The moment I speak out against homosexuality, I'm denounced as a bigot."

"By people who perceive your words as bigoted."

"In other words, there is an increasing cultural prejudice against Christianity."

"Or an increasing consensus about the harmful effects of homophobia. Do you really want to chain Christianity to a defense of discrimination against LGBTQ people? There are Christian congregations that would take strong exception to that. Which means it's not even a Christian belief you're defending; it's a sectarian belief. But in a sane country, no particular sect is allowed to write its doctrines into law."

Chris shifts in his chair. He glances at the window, where, because he is imaginary, he sees no reflection of himself. The street lights have winked on now, and their orange glow smolders through a scrim of falling snow.

"Fine. Set aside legislation. Does your version of atheism at least make possible a polite discourse between atheists and Christians?"

"Polite discourse has always been possible. Historically, it hasn't been atheists who shut that discourse down."

"I'm thinking of the so-called New Atheists, and especially online atheists—the head lice of the internet. Their obnoxious memes, their conspicuous ignorance of the philosophical tradition, their facile dismissal of centuries of Christian thought. Their smug incredulity!—as if Christians were nothing but a gang of Darwin-hating, gay-baiting, science-denying Neanderthals."

"We don't speak ill of Neanderthals in this house, Chris."

"Very funny. But you know what I mean."

"Of course I do. And the last thing I want to do is defend ignorance or arrogance. The internet is a garden where many things grow, and most of them aren't flowers. So we agree about that."

"Good."

"But can I say a word in defense of the incredulity of naïve atheists?"

"I'm powerless to stop you."

"I think much of that incredulity is legitimate, even if it's misdirected. Suppose you tell me that Jesus was resurrected after his death—"

"I *do* tell you that Jesus was resurrected after his death."

"And suppose I react with incredulity. Is that incredulity justified?"

"Not from where I sit. In the context of my worldview, the resurrection makes perfect sense."

"So maybe the naïve atheist's incredulity is aimed at the wrong target. Maybe what inspires her incredulity isn't the resurrection story itself, but your expectation that she should accept it as an established truth."

"I consider it an established truth."

"But our atheist doesn't share your metaphysical beliefs, and in the absence of your metaphysical beliefs all she has is a story and some Bayesian priors. And her Bayesian priors strongly suggest that stories about people rising from the grave are consistently fictional or mythical. The idea that she ought to grant historical status to Biblical miracle stories constitutes a kind of Christian privilege. It only makes sense inside a Christian bubble. And we don't live in that bubble. And you *know* we don't live in that bubble. So if you want to tell us Jesus rose from the dead, or that he chatted with Moses and Elijah, or that he cast demons into a herd of swine . . . you really shouldn't be surprised if we react with incredulity."

Chris sighs and shakes his head. "I'm well past being surprised by the incredulity of atheists."

* * *

2. Are you ruling out testimony as a source of knowledge?

"Back to your 'inventory of knowledge'," Chris says. "Do you admit that my inventory of knowledge might be different from yours?"

"I'm sure it is! Everyone's state of knowledge is unique. Like snowflakes."

Snowflakes flutter past the window, collect in soft mounds on the sill.

"You talk a lot about evidence, and how we make Bayesian estimates of probability, and so on. But that's facile. Not all knowledge comes to us in a neat Bayesian package. What about other sources of knowledge?"

I've brewed a pot of coffee, which Chris is too stubbornly imaginary to enjoy, and we pause while I pour myself a cup. "Okay, other sources of knowledge . . . such as?"

"Testimony. Or immediate experience."

"Take those one at a time. You're saying testimony is a source of knowledge about metaphysical reality?"

"I'm saying testimony is a source of knowledge about many things. We learn from each other—that's what human beings do. Have you ever measured the mass of an electron? No? But you're perfectly willing to take the word of a physicist about it."

"I am. And I'm aware that 'testimony' is one of those issues philosophers of knowledge wrangle about. But let's make a caveat here. I'm willing to take the word of a physicist about the mass of an electron, in part because I know from experience that physicists study such things and that they usually report their findings in good faith. In effect, I'm placing a bet that the physicist knows what he's talking about. And at least in principle, I could perform the same tests and make the same calculations a physicist would use to determine the mass of an electron, as anyone could; the process isn't hidden. All the Bayesian priors for my confidence in the testimony of physicists are in place. But you're not talking about physics, really, are you? You're talking about confidence in the testimony of your faith community, or the testimony of ecclesiastical tradition, or the testimony of the authors of Biblical texts—right?"

"Ultimately, yes."

"Which is a very different kettle of Bayesian fish."

"But wait a minute—you've said yourself that metaphysical beliefs don't come with a lot of Bayesian priors."

"Sure. But it's not the metaphysical claims that are in question now, it's the reliability of the claimant's testimony. When it comes to metaphysical knowledge, should I defer to a Christian, a Buddhist, a Taoist, the Apostle Paul, or the guy down the street who has dreams about angels? All of the above? None of the above?"

"I can accept the tenets of my faith community without evidence, if I choose to, at least in the absence of compelling evidence *against* them."

"Of course you can! But for the same reason, you can't reasonably expect *me* to accept them."

"Okay. But again, that seems facile. This isn't 'the guy down the street who has dreams about angels.' You're casually dismissing a faith with millions of adherents and a doctrinal tradition that has endured for almost two millennia."

"More than one faith has those credentials."

"And there is the testimony of the Gospels, more fundamentally."

"To which the same objection applies."

"Does it? I'm convinced the Gospels are reliable accounts of a genuine divine intervention in human history."

"And I'm sure that's an accurate description of your belief. But—and I mean no offense—I'm not convinced that *you're* a reliable source of knowledge about divine interventions in human history."

"It's not just me—I don't make this claim purely on my behalf."

"But I'm hearing it from you. If it's testimony, it has to come from *someone*. Right now I'm getting it from you. Some days I get it from the Jehovah's Witnesses at my door, or from the Eastern Orthodox family down the block, or from the guy handing out tracts outside the local mosque. All of whom, presumably, got it in turn from other sources. But the buck has to stop somewhere. How far back does your chain of testimony go? To the Council of Nicaea? The letters of St. Paul?"

"As I said, the Gospels—"

"But there are all kinds of ways of reading the Gospels. Lots of competing interpretations of scripture. Are you saying your interpretation is the authoritative one?"

"I'm as fallible as anyone else—"

"Exactly."

"But—well, dammit, you've made your own knowledge claim, whether you admit it or not! 'It's extraordinarily unlikely that God exists.' How is that any different?"

"What I'm saying is that it's extraordinarily unlikely that any single one of all the countless potential descriptions of metaphysical reality is the correct one. Maybe yours *is* the lottery winner. Maybe you, or your pastor, or Eustathius of Antioch, or the authors of the Book of Genesis, reached into the cosmically large jar of jellybeans and pulled out the One True Jellybean. But I have no way of knowing that, and I can't reasonably or honestly accept your testimony at face value."

* * *

3. Isn't personal religious experience a legitimate source of knowledge?

Outside, in the dimming of the day, tree branches bow in jagged arcs under a freight of snow. Someone nearby is shoveling a driveway. The blade of the shovel scrapes asphalt in a muted, periodic groan.

Chris stands and paces unhappily. "Your book," he says at last, "appears to be about atheism as a lived experience—a state of knowledge, if you like—rather than a philosophical proposition. But Christianity is a lived experience too, and you don't seem to want to acknowledge that. Divine revelation, the indwelling of the Holy Spirit, religious experience in general: those aren't just empty words. They're the substance from which some of us construct our lives. They sustain our love for others and our hope for a better future. They connect us with something infinitely larger and more mysterious than ourselves. I mean, look outside—"

"It's cold and windy, and it's getting dark."

"It's cold and windy and it's almost Christmas, a time when Christians celebrate the entry into the world of a kind of redemptive magic—love and mercy more wonderful than our minds can encompass. Maybe you're deaf to that, but I'm not. Don't you think it's remarkable that a simple story about a peasant child born in Bethlehem has echoed down so many centuries?"

Across the street, a neighbor's Christmas decorations bleed bright color into the snow-gray evening. "It *is* remarkable."

"Then let me anticipate your answer. You'll tell me subjective experience carries no interpersonal weight. You'll tell me people of all faiths have had similar experiences but interpret them very differently."

"More or less. It's not the experience I'm questioning, it's the spin. A sense of oceanic peace, or of the presence of some transcendent being, no matter how genuine or how profoundly felt, doesn't confer expertise about metaphysical reality—or, *if* it does, there's no way to *demonstrate* that it does, no rational way to choose between competing claims about such experiences."

"Are you so absolutely sure of your own state of knowledge?"

"Actually I'm not. I can fairly readily be convinced that I know less than I think I do. It's happened to me more often than I care to admit. But it's much harder to convince me I *do* know something when, in fact, I don't. And one of the truest things I can say about myself is that I don't know anything about the nature of ultimate reality."

"What would you have us do, then, those of us who hear that music in our hearts? We can defend it with philosophy, we can point to signs and wonders in the natural world, but the experience itself is fundamentally ineffable—beyond speaking. 'No eye has seen, no ear has heard, no heart has imagined what God has prepared for those who love Him.' Are we supposed to abandon that promise in favor of, what . . . some barren, Nietzschean wasteland? A joyless cosmology, drained of all significance? Nothing for solace or redemption but whatever shallow comfort we can eke out of a few brief decades of physical existence?"

"I'm not asking you to do that."

"How do you see it, then? C.S. Lewis once wrote about the human yearning for the presence of God—he compared it to 'the scent of a flower we have not found, the echo of a tune we have not heard, news from a country we have never visited.' He called it a secret, a secret that pierces with its sweetness. 'We cannot hide it,' he said, 'because our experience is constantly suggesting it.' What place does that yearning have—what place does the human heart and its turning toward the eternal have—in your unknowable, godless universe?"

The light is fading quickly, and so is Chris. Like all imaginary things, he is elusive. He loses definition; he begins to dissolve into the shadows creeping from the corners of the room. His last words are a soft diminuendo:

I deserve an answer!

And he's right. He does.

9

Owning the Unknown

The worn tired stars say
you shall die early and die dirty.
The clean cold stars say
you shall die late and die clean.
The runaway stars say
you shall never die at all,
never at all.

—Carl Sandburg, *Slabs of the Sunburnt West*

The mirror weighed one and a half tons and measured 200 inches in diameter. No mirror of its size and precision had ever before been manufactured, and its construction tested the limits of contemporary technology. The mirror was cast as a single disc of borosilicate glass at the Corning Glass Works in New York State in December of 1935; the Corning factory maintained the glass in its molten state in the annealing oven for another month, then reduced the heat incrementally until, more than ten months later, the mirror reached ambient temperature and was ready to be shipped.

In March of 1936 the mirror was packed into a fifteen-ton steel crate lined with layers of absorbent material and placed on a specially-designed rail car. The train assembled to transport the mirror consisted of a locomotive, the rail car, a tender carrying ancillary equipment, and a caboose. For most of its journey of more than 3,000 miles, the train traveled at speeds of less than thirty miles per hour. Across the country, as the train inched through Buffalo, Cleveland, St. Louis, Kansas City, and on through the desolate American southwest, curiosity-seekers lined the tracks to see it pass. On April 11, the mirror arrived at the Caltech optical shop in Pasadena, California. At Caltech the mirror was laboriously ground and polished into a final paraboloid shape, its contours measured in wavelengths of light, a process that would take—with war delays—another eleven and a half years.

On November 16, 1947, the mirror was loaded onto a heavily-reinforced semitrailer for its final journey from Caltech to Palomar Mountain in the Peninsular Ranges of northern San Diego County. Where necessary, roads had been widened and bridges reinforced to accommodate the sixty-ton vehicle. The truck, accompanied for much of its journey by a motorcade of Highway Patrolmen, burned a gallon of gasoline every three miles and had to be repeatedly refueled en route. A dedicated road, dubbed the Highway to the Stars, had been constructed from the city of Escondido to the summit of Mount Palomar, with just enough room for the truck and cargo to clear its sinuous twists and turns. On November 19 the mirror arrived intact at the construction site of the Palomar Observatory, where—after another two years of installation, adjustment, and final polishing—it became the key element in what was then the largest optical telescope in the world.

The Hale Telescope was a successor and companion to the 100-inch Hooker telescope on Mount Wilson. The Hooker telescope had seen first light in 1917, on the brink of the First World War, and the ceremonies at its inauguration had celebrated both the grandeur of the skies and the triumphs of science. Thirty years and two world wars later, the dedication of the Hale Telescope was a more haunted, chastened affair. In June of 1948 more than 800 guests crowded together under the observatory dome—literally in the shadow of the huge mirror assembly—for a ceremony hosted by Caltech President Lee A. DuBridge. A printed program of the event began with the canticle *Benedicte, Omnia Opera Dei* from the Book of Common Prayer, continued with the text of five speeches (one by Vannevar Bush, who had played a critical role in the Manhattan Project that created the fission weapons dropped on Hiroshima and Nagasaki), and concluded with Psalms VIII, 3–5 ("What is man that thou art mindful of him?").

The war, the atomic bomb, and the fate of humanity were much on the mind of the dignitaries who spoke at the dedication. The President of the Rockefeller Foundation, Raymond Fosdick, began by citing "the shattering events of the last two decades. . . . Knowledge and destruction have joined in a Grand Alliance that has made the history of our generation a history of deepening horror." The dedication of the telescope, he said, has brought us "face to face with the problem of the unpredictable consequences of knowledge. We cannot even guess what will come from this mighty instrument, or to what ends the fresh insights which we gain here will be employed." But in the end he was cautiously optimistic about the possibilities the telescope presented:

This great new window to the stars will bring us into touch with those outposts of time and space which have beckoned from immemorial ages. It will bring into fresh focus the mystery of the universe, its order, its beauty, its power. It will dramatize the questions which mankind has always asked and to which no answers have been found, and perhaps can ever be found. Why are we here on this dwarf planet? Are there other planets that have burst into consciousness like our own? Is there an

answering intelligence anywhere in space? Is there purpose behind the apparent meaninglessness and incomprehensibility of
the universe? What is this divine spark of awareness which we
call consciousness? And finally, in the words and spirit of the
Psalmist, what is man?[1]

Vannevar Bush took up some of the same themes in his speech.
Astronomy, he said, was a unique science:

> In no other discipline ... do men confront mystery and chal-
> lenge of the order of that which looms down upon the astron-
> omer in the long watches of the night. The astronomer knows
> at first hand, and places the rest of us in his lasting debt by
> translating to us, how slight is our Earth, how slight and fleet-
> ing are mankind. But more than that, he senses more closely
> than we can, I think, the majesty which resides in the mind of
> man because that mind seeks in all its slightness to see, to learn,
> to understand at least some little part of the mysterious majesty
> of the universe. No calling brings more sharply into focus the
> seeming disparity between man and the cosmos. And yet, no
> calling reflects more steadily the fact, both prideful and hum-
> bling at once, that the reaches of the intelligence of man are vast
> and that his will strives to extend them to encompass even the
> fabulous reaches beyond the stars.[2]

In January of 1949 the astronomer Edwin Hubble made the
first photographic exposure through the telescope. It was an im-
age of an object with the catalog number NGC 2261, otherwise
known as Hubble's Variable Nebula. (This was the same Hubble
in whose honor the orbiting Hubble Space Telescope would be
named, many years later.) By the beginning of the 1950s, the public's fascination with astronomy had spread in concentric ripples
from the Palomar Observatory. Among Hubble's circle of friends
was the English expatriate writer Aldous Huxley, author of the
speculative-fiction classic *Brave New World*, who had lately associated himself with the Vedanta Society of Southern California,

and whose interest in mysticism would lead him to a series of experiments with the psychedelic drug mescaline, the subject of his 1954 book *The Doors of Perception*. And at the foot of Palomar Mountain, George Adamski, a one-time theosophist and occultist who had made money during the Prohibition era by producing and retailing wine "for religious purposes," had recently purchased 20 acres of land. In addition to building a campground and a roadside restaurant called the Palomar Gardens Café, Adamski sensed fresh money-making possibilities in the first newspaper reports of unidentified flying objects—"flying saucers," in the vernacular of the day. He quickly achieved notoriety (and a continuing source of income) by faking photographs of alleged flying objects, which he claimed carried visitors from other worlds, and which he constructed from such mundane objects as surgical lamps and light bulbs.

* * *

In this convergence of ideas and impulses we can see a glimmer of things to come. Most of the elements of the 1960s youth insurgency in America are already present, sometimes explicitly, in the constellation of personalities that interacted around Edwin Hubble and the Palomar Observatory in the late 1940s: an anti-war impulse, the fear of a coldly over-reaching scientism, psychedelic drugs, second-hand mysticism, and a certain expansive if not necessarily well-considered credulity. Add a copy of Thoreau's *Walden* and a vinyl pressing of *Sergeant Pepper's Lonely Hearts Club Band*, and you have 1967 in a nutshell.

The literary genre that reacted most immediately to this emerging cultural nexus was, of course, science fiction. And, via science fiction, some of these same ideas helped shape my own work in the genre and fostered a lifelong engagement with them. If you've wondered why a science fiction author is writing about God—in this book or any other—you can find the beginning of an answer here.

God, gods, beings largely indistinguishable from gods, and advanced civilizations with godlike powers became a staple in postwar and contemporary science fiction, as did concerns about the fate of mankind in the aftermath of Hiroshima and Nagasaki. Arthur C. Clarke's *Childhood's End* (1953) envisions an Earth transformed by powerful aliens who help create a golden age without war or poverty, until entities even more powerful arrive with other ideas. Similarly, the 1951 film *The Day the Earth Stood Still* imagines a galactic federation of worlds offering humanity a blunt ultimatum: put aside your childish impulse to make war, or be destroyed. The 1956 film *Forbidden Planet* raises questions about the ultimate purpose and limits of technology: an alien civilization that has perfected its technology faces destruction when its own unconscious, irrational impulses gain access to godlike power. The novel *A Case of Conscience* (1958) by James Blish portrays a Jesuit cleric of the far future, perplexed when he encounters aliens who behave with an innate sense of morality but possess no religious beliefs. The science fiction writer Roger Zelazny literalized the Hindu pantheon of deities on a distant colony world of the future in his 1967 novel *Lord of Light*. Stanley Kubrick's *2001: A Space Odyssey* transformed another story by Arthur C. Clarke, 1951's "The Sentinel," into a meditation on human destiny that climaxes in an orgy of visionary images, as if the evolutionary theology of Pierre Tielhard de Chardin had been compressed into an acid-drenched sugar cube.

The science-fictional engagement with religion began before and continued long after the 1960s. Consider James Morrow's 1994 novel *Towing Jehovah* with its memorable first line: "The irreducible strangeness of the universe was first made manifest to Anthony Van Horne on his fiftieth birthday, when a despondent angel named Raphael, a being with luminous white wings and a halo that blinked on and off like a neon quoit, appeared and told him of the days to come."[3] (The angel explains that God has died and fallen into the sea; Van Horne will captain the vessel tasked with towing the two-mile-long divine corpse into Arctic waters, where the icy water will help preserve it from decay.) Angels of a more terrifying sort—capricious, unpredictable, often deadly—appear in Ted Chiang's 2001 short story "Hell is the Absence of God." ("It was an unexceptional visitation, smaller in magnitude than most but no different in kind, bringing blessings to some and disaster to others. In this instance the angel was Nathanael, making an appearance in a downtown shopping district." The protagonist's wife Sarah is part of the collateral damage, "hit by flying glass when the angel's billowing curtain of flame shattered the storefront window of the café in which she was eating.")⁴ And in Robert J. Sawyer's 2000 novel *Calculating God*, spider-like alien visitors arrive at a Canadian museum to examine its fossil collection, hoping to find evidence for their belief that the universe was designed by a God-like being—much to the dismay of the novel's protagonist, a paleontologist and atheist named Thomas Jericho.

Defining "science fiction" is a game the genre's fans and critics have been playing since at least the era of the early pulp magazines, probably best summed up (and dismissed) by the writer Damon Knight's remark that science fiction "means what we point to when we say it." Nevertheless, over the years, I've ventured a couple of definitions of my own—playful descriptions more than definitions—that might help explain why the genre so often seems to be performing an awkward *pas de deux* with religion.

In one of these definitions, I called science fiction "the miracle stories of the Enlightenment." Miracle stories—stories of miracle-workers, divine visitations, strange and distant lands and creatures—are abundant in classical and European literature, from the *Odyssey* to *Beowulf* to Dante's *Divine Comedy*, and in storytelling and mythic traditions from every other part of the world. An example from the Christian tradition is the *Infancy Gospel of Thomas*, an apocryphal text, declared heretical by the fourth-century church historian Eusebius, that narrates the life of Jesus as a child.

In the *Infancy Gospel*, the pre-pubescent Jesus fashions a flock of clay birds and causes them to fly; in another episode he brings a dried fish from the marketplace back to life. In one sequence Jesus kills another child by cursing him and blinds the child's parents when they complain—an act the elder Jesus might have thought better of—then astonishes a would-be teacher by resurrecting the dead child and healing the blinded parents. The premise of a dangerously powerful child learning, or failing to learn, to control his powers is a perennially fascinating one, and it shouldn't be surprising that early Christians invented their own versions.

The Enlightenment set back European Christianity a few paces by lending priority to human experience and secular reason, a perspective that cast Christianized miracle stories in a new and less flattering light. But it did nothing to allay the appetite for such stories, and the perceptible advances of science and technology during the Industrial Revolution made it possible to transplant miracle stories into a more Enlightenment-friendly ontology. Mary Shelley's 1818 novel *Frankenstein* is a story infused with classical and religious imagery—"I ought to be thy Adam," the monster tells its creator, "but I am rather the fallen angel"—but its central miracle is enabled by medical and physical science. More than half a century later, H. G. Wells and his literary heirs found room for their miracles in a consistently secular context. In these stories the heavens are populated, but not by ghosts or gods; artificial beings are animated by clever machinery, not magic spells; humans fly to the moon in spaceships, not in chariots pulled by swans. In effect, science fiction traded the *Infancy Gospel of Thomas* for *Village of the Damned*, the *Odyssey* for a Space Odyssey. And while we still read miracle stories of a less ontologically rigorous kind—think *Lord of the Rings* or *Game of Thrones*—we generally call them "fantasy."

The other definition of science fiction I offered was that it is "the literature of human contingency." In less academic words, science fiction is a literature inextricably entangled with the reality of change. By setting stories in the future, in the remote past, and in alternate histories, virtually every science fiction story implicitly restates at least one of three fundamental propositions: *Our world was once a very different place. The world as we know it might have been a very different place, if things had happened differently. And the world, in time, will become a very different place from the world as it is now.*

These may seem like self-evident truisms, but they're not necessarily comfortable ones. They aren't entirely absent from mainstream literature—Proust's *Remembrance of Things Past* has a few things to say about how the world changes around us—but science fiction pushes the scale past a human lifetime and implicates not just our daily experience but our entire universe. H. G. Wells reminds us that London was once a river valley roamed by wooly mammoths. Philip K. Dick, in his novel *The Man in the High Castle*, suggests that a different Second World War could have left Americans living in a conquered nation. Kim Stanley Robinson's *Mars* trilogy knows that as humanity's place in the solar system changes, the way we organize human societies and economies will evolve along with it. And so on.

This is the view from science fiction. For some of us the perspective is intoxicating, even addictive. For others it might seem vertiginous. Some of the first celebrity visitors to Palomar, allowed to peer through the eyepiece of the Hale Telescope, had a similar reaction. Were these flecks of ancient starlight, collected and brought into focus by the Hale's huge mirror, a vision of limitless grandeur or a glimpse into a lifeless, inhuman void?

For established monotheisms like Christianity there will inevitably be a hint of the heretical in all this talk of time and change. The Vatican has its own observatory and is reconciled to the dispensations of contemporary astronomy, but its view of history is fixed and teleological. We were made in a garden, we fell from grace, and a divine redeemer has shown us the path to an eternal kingdom. There are revealed truths, in other words, that mark us as something more than contingent creatures. If God inexplicably failed to place us at the center of the universe, at least he gives us his full attention.

This, I think, is what Christians mean when they talk about the cold, unforgiving universe implied by atheism: an uncentered and ungoverned cosmos in which human beings are a recent and transient phenomenon, without divine precedent or heavenly destiny. "A flicker in one day of the lives of stars," as the science fiction writer Olaf Stapledon said.[5] "A barren, Nietzschean wasteland," as my imaginary interlocutor Chris described it in the previous chapter.

But if that's the case—if atheism has thrown out all the babies along with the metaphysical bathwater—what does it mean to live a life apart from the consolations of revealed religion?

* * *

One of my earliest memories is of badgering my parents, during a car trip across the country from California to Pennsylvania, to undertake a detour to the Barringer meteor crater in the Arizona desert east of Flagstaff.

I was seven years old, and the Barringer crater—officially named simply "Meteor Crater," formerly and more evocatively known as the Canyon Diablo Crater, and commonly called Barringer after the family that owned the land—had been in the news lately. For years the scientific consensus had been that the site was an ancient volcanic caldera, but a steady accumulation of new evidence had challenged that conclusion. The discovery at the Barringer site of the mineral coesite, a compressed quartz produced in high-energy impacts, clinched the argument, and an article in the July 1960 issue of *Science* by the geologist Eugene Shoemaker and others made a decisive case that the crater had resulted from a meteor impact during the Pleistocene era, roughly 50,000 years ago. Local California newspapers and television stations reported the discovery, which is likely where I first heard of it.

From those reports I would have learned another surprising thing: in the cooler and wetter climate of the Pleistocene, what was now desert had been a lightly forested prairie supporting a diverse animal population, including mammoths, tapirs, and giant ground sloths. And so, in the summer of 1960, as we veered off Route 66 and followed tourist signage toward the crater, I tried to picture that vanished landscape—junipers and pinyon pines climbing the slopes of the brown hills that now corrugated the horizon, a gentle breeze combing meadows of grass and wildflowers where today it stirred up whirlwinds of alkaline dust. What was even better, after we had parked and paid admission, and as I hurried ahead of my parents to the viewing platform at the edge of the crater, was imagining the impact itself. A nickel-iron rock roughly fifty meters wide had shed half its mass as it boiled through the atmosphere at 12.8 kilometers per second, carving a luminous slash across an ancient noon or midnight sky, silent until it struck the earth in an explosion equivalent to the detonation of a 10-megaton nuclear bomb. The comparison was timely. In 1952 the United States had exploded a 10-megaton hydrogen bomb in the Pacific as part of its ongoing nuclear weapons tests; the bomb had vaporized Elugelab Island and sent a mushroom cloud thirty miles into the stratosphere. Any living thing near the Barringer meteor impact would have been instantly killed or horrifically injured, to a radius of more than thirty kilometers from the blast site. As a child I didn't know and wouldn't have understood the numbers modern science assigns to that impact, but the picture was vivid in my mind. All this had happened, really happened, and it had happened here, right here where I stood, and it had blasted a hole fifty stories deep and more than half a mile wide into the sleepy Pleistocene meadowlands, a hole that still existed all these millennia later, long after the creeks and rivers had dried up, long after the desert had devoured the forests, long after the mammoths had given way to a tribe of clever hominins who marked the spot with a paved road, a string of Burma-Shave signs, and a gift shop.

My parents had to pry me away. They wanted to make Albuquerque before dark.

It's probably unusual for a seven-year-old to obsess over a geological feature, but I don't want to leave the impression that I was some kind of intellectual prodigy. I knew a few things, and I was a precocious reader, but my understanding of human history would have been something like "cavemen, Romans, knights, cowboys, the present." What made our visit to the Barringer crater memorable was the strange, sweet pleasure of knowing that the physical world had changed so radically, of seeing the evidence of a wildly different past gouged into the sun-shot stillness of the Arizona desert. It was like learning a wonderful secret, like suddenly understanding that ice and water and fog are all one substance. This was not the apocalyptic vision of Isaiah 40:4, "Every valley shall be lifted up, and every mountain and hill be made low; the uneven ground shall become level, and the rough places a plain." It was not "All flesh is grass, and all its glory like the flowers of the field." It was a glimpse of something much more impersonal, a tide of change that operated not just in the human world but inexorably, if invisibly, in rocks, in sand, in the stars themselves.

I couldn't have articulated what I felt that day, but, in a way, my career as a writer has been a prolonged attempt to do just that. You can find it reflected, subtly or overtly, in most of my novels and short stories. In "Divided by Infinity" (1998), a man makes the horrifying discovery that he cannot die but can only transition into a series of increasingly less likely universes in which his life somehow continues despite the odds against it. He arrives at last at a desiccated far-future Earth—a landscape not unlike the high Arizona desert—where he is subsumed into an alien existence he could never have anticipated. In "The Observer" (1998), included in the appendix to this book, I imagined a troubled young girl of the 1950s visiting an uncle who is part of the astronomer Edwin Hubble's circle of celebrity friends, as she struggles to come to terms with some decidedly non-ordinary visionary experiences. *Spin* (2005) is probably my most successful attempt to explore these ideas at novel length and is my most widely-read and widely-translated book. *Spin* encloses the earth itself in a kind of planet-wide time machine: for every year that passes on Earth more than a hundred million years pass in the exterior universe, bringing the evolution of stars, including the lethal expansion of our own sun, into the lifespan of contemporary human beings.

The apparently godless universe of late-twentieth-century scientific cosmology has never seemed to me hostile or terrifying. Mysterious, yes; impersonal, yes; astonishingly vast, yes indeed. Remarkable, certainly, in the way it encompasses a deep and enfolding strangeness, so that the four borders of the observable universe—the primordial past, the implicate future, the very large, the very small—are also the borders of human understanding. The "godless universe" is and has been for most of my life the source of a profound and enduring personal pleasure, the pleasure of standing outside myself and seeing not just the present moment but the evolving string of moments that unwind into the darkness before and after it.

* * *

But maybe this elides the most obvious component of Chris's objection to an atheistic cosmos—the human knowledge of death.

It's impossible to deny that we're a species haunted by the specter of mortality, and I'm not the sort of atheist who derides Christianity as a foolish way of coping with the awareness of death. In one way or another, we all shield ourselves from that knowledge. The death of ourselves and our loved ones is not something most of us can comfortably imagine. We instinctively distance ourselves from it, because living with it as an immediate truth would be psychologically intolerable. People exposed to death on a daily basis—combat veterans, war refugees, first responders, health care professionals—are at enormously heightened risk for stress disorders, for reasons that aren't hard to understand. We "discount the future," as economists say, because the future, in the end, is lethal. And, naturally enough, we tell ourselves stories to allay our fears. Atheism in this view threatens to steal those consoling stories and leave nothing in their place but a blunt, brutal realism—the spiritual equivalent of Stalinist architecture.

Against this, it's important to understand what atheism does *not* require us to renounce. Atheists can freely acknowledge the profundity and significance of mythic and religious art and narrative. An atheist can look at the Shah Mosque in Isfahan, its walls and ceilings adorned with 475,000 tiles arranged in breathtakingly intricate spiraling mosaics, and feel its power to draw us away from the constraints of ordinary consciousness. Atheists are quite capable of understanding the attraction of a story about a divinely-conceived child who promises his followers an ultimate redemption, who is tortured and killed by a cruel and uncomprehending political establishment, and who rises miraculously from the tomb to which his body has been consigned. Atheists know that what the psychologist William James called "the religious experience" is a real phenomenon, and some of us have experienced it personally. The cultural fascination with psychedelics that began with Aldous Huxley's 1953 mescaline trip arrived at my doorstep belatedly and only briefly—and many theists will immediately object that a chemically-induced religious experience is either counterfeit or inauthentic, "barging into the presence of God" as the theologian Richard Swinburne described it—but I do know what it is to feel an ineffable personal connection to the unfolding of the world and to experience, at least momentarily, a peace that surpasses understanding. Equally, the theist shares the atheist's experience of grief, injustice, rage, sorrow, and loss. Even the Christian who insists God is not indifferent to suffering knows that human beings too often are; even the Christian who believes there is solace in heaven understands that far too many of us fail to find it here on earth.

These are human universals. None of us is exempt.

And how consoling, really, is Christian theism? Would it be comforting to believe human consciousness somehow survives death? I'm not sure it would, because I don't know what that might mean. The idea of being reunited with lost loved ones, the idea of a bodily resurrection in a perfected world, is obviously attractive. But that's not quite what Christian doctrine promises. In the Christian afterlife, rewards are conditional and punishments are potentially dire. There's nothing remotely reassuring in the thought that a beloved friend or family member might be excluded from paradise, or annihilated, or even consigned to eternal conscious torment, simply because she drew the wrong conclusion about which notional God to worship. It implies a God who is not only all-powerful but vengeful, narcissistic, and monstrously petty. And that, in turn, implies a cosmos colder and more fundamentally horrifying than any supposed "void."

* * *

In a recent book, *How God Becomes Real*, Stanford anthropologist T.M. Luhrmann describes her research on spiritual practices, particularly in American evangelism but also in the charismatic Christian sects of West Africa and India and in the West Indian Santería religion. Her book has much to say about the function of prayer and ritual in those belief systems and the therapeutic effects they might have, but she deliberately sets aside the question of whether these worshippers are in fact communicating with a real God or gods. "The puzzle of religion," as she describes it, "is not the problem of false belief but the question of how gods and spirits become and remain real to people and what this real-making does for humans." Ritual, ceremony, and praxis, in her view, are ways of deliberately fostering a sense of the reality of immaterial beings who matter "in the here and now. . . . For humans to sustain their involvement with entities who are invisible and matter in a good way to their lives, I suggest that a god must be made real again and again against the evident features of an obdurate world. Humans must somehow be brought to a point from which the altar becomes more than gilded wood, so that the icon's eyes look back at them, ablaze."[6]

There is nothing in this that would surprise Eudena, our ambassador from the Paleolithic. "The passage from the daylight world to the shadow world can't be opened on a whim," she reminds us. "You need a fire, a song, a shaman, a sacred plant—this is obvious. How foolish to think otherwise."

So should we set aside the question of God's existence and let his devotees get on with the potentially therapeutic business of imagining him into their lives?

Perhaps, but "the problem of false belief" is not so easily dodged. There is a price to be paid for denying "the evident features of an obdurate world," even as a means to a laudable or reasonable end—perhaps especially so in the twenty-first century, when the light reflected in the icon's eyes comes less often from a communal fire and more often from the glow of a smartphone linked to a sketchy website.

Toxic credulity has become a conspicuous threat to democratic governance in the first quarter of this century. In January of 2021, bizarre online conspiracy theories and a deliberately propagated lie about the American presidential election culminated in a deadly assault on the United States Capitol building in Washington, D.C., with consequences that have yet to play out. Much ink has been spilled on the subject of how these ideas arise, how they spread, and how they motivate those who hold them to commit crimes up to and including sedition and murder. I think it's plausible to suggest that some of this follows from the dynamics of denialism in an age of social media.

The deliberate, concerted, and systematic denial of an obvious truth is a practice hardly unique to organized religion. Much of American history has unfolded under the shadow of a foundational denialism: the refusal to accept that the ideals expressed in the Constitution and the Declaration of Independence are irreconcilable with a system of racialized human captivity and forced labor; a denial, even after the Civil War and the legal abolition of slavery, that that system was in any way immoral or inhumane. Over the course of two hundred years, some Christians have lent support to that denialism and other Christians have devoted at least as much effort to exposing and condemning it. We can identify more recent denialisms that are entirely secular in nature: the refusal to accept that smoking is carcinogenic, say, or the campaign to deny that the burning of fossil fuels causes global climate change. One particularly persistent brand of Christian denialism—Christian in the sense that it originated with and is sustained by self-identified Christians—is the denial that life on Earth evolved from simpler forms over millions of years. The problem for people who espouse such systems of denial is that in order to protect a cherished belief from contradiction, they need to wall themselves off from more reliable sources of knowledge. The effect of that isolation, in an age of online social networks, is to put them in contact with and lend a specious credibility to all the adjacent denialisms that thrive wherever evidence is systematically derided or suppressed. Spend much time in digital spaces devoted to young-Earth creationism, for instance, and you'll soon enough be exposed to global-warming denialists, anti-vaxxers, Holocaust deniers, people who insist that the condensation trails from high-flying aircraft are "chemtrails," people who believe certain political and cultural figures are actually extraterrestrial lizard creatures disguised as human—and so on. The net result, as I write this, is a pandemic of credulity, an increasingly large community of people whose immunity to misinformation has been compromised and who are exposed to an exponentially multiplying tangle of malicious falsehoods virulent enough to shake the foundations of even long-established parliamentary democracies.

There are a couple of lessons we can draw from this. One is

that "the problem of false belief" shouldn't be casually dismissed. We do ourselves no favor by failing to draw sharp lines between what might be true, what we hope to be true, what we believe to be true, and what we simply don't know.

Too often we treat an admission of ignorance as a confession of weakness, and even atheists are occasionally caught claiming that religious beliefs must be false because science has already answered all the important questions. But that gets it exactly backward. Science has *not* answered all the important questions, and "I don't know" is often the truest and most honest thing we can say about ourselves. An atheism framed as knowledge about absolute reality is nothing but theism in a mirror. An atheism that follows from an admitted lack of metaphysical knowledge is more solidly grounded and, in the end, far more defensible.

The second lesson we can draw is a humbling one, especially for a novelist. It's about the nature of stories.

University of Utah anthropologist Polly Weissner has spent decades studying the Ju/'hoansi hunter-gatherers of Southern Africa, documenting the content of their daily conversation, and one of her most intriguing discoveries is that, by daylight, "about one third of discussions concerned practical topics such as hunting strategies and technology, for instance, with another third devoted to complaints about group members." At night, however, "around 80 percent of conversations were in the form of stories. Some were funny, others exciting—all were entertaining. Yet they often also contained information about social etiquette and tradition, as well as about geographically distant social contacts who could be visited for help during times of hardship. In other words, listening to these stories had the potential to make life and survival easier." In the big picture, according to Weissner, "stories are probably more important than day talk."[7]

For nearly forty years I have told stories for a living. Many of those stories fall into the categories we identified in chapter three, stories of dual ontology and the disembodied self. Some are door-in-the-wall stories. Some are ghost stories in all but name. Their effectiveness depends in part on our predisposition to engage emotionally and imaginatively with such narratives, to enter into them as if into a dream and to suspend our disbelief for as long as our eyes are on the page. For the storyteller, and for the storyteller's audience, the human capacity for enchantment is evolution's gift—a feature, not a bug. Today we have a wealth of stories at our fingertips, not just in the written word but in live performances and on large and small screens, and most of us find at least some of those stories to be moving, meaningful, life-enhancing, or at least enjoyable. And like the stories of the Ju/'hoansi people, our stories serve more than one purpose. The novelist George Eliot said art has the ability to "enlarge men's sympathies," and recent research has confirmed her intuition. "Psychologists Mar and Keith Oatley tested the idea that entering fiction's simulated social worlds enhances our ability to connect with actual human beings," according to a 2012 article in the *Boston Globe*, and they found that "heavy fiction readers outperformed heavy nonfiction readers on tests of empathy, even after they controlled for the possibility that people who already had high empathy might naturally gravitate to fiction. As Oatley puts it, fiction serves the function of 'making the world a better place by improving interpersonal understanding'."[8]

But fiction, as we think of it, is a relatively recent invention. Human beings wrestled with the problem of false belief for centuries before we learned to draw the distinctions we take for granted today—to disentangle fiction from myth, history from legend, biography from hagiography, theater from ritual, philosophy from dogma, medicine from magic, astronomy from astrology. By doing so we opened up vast new possibility spaces, not just in the sciences but in the humanities and the arts. Making these distinctions isn't in any sense a disenchantment of the world. It isn't an aggressive scientism that hollows out the world's mysteries. On the contrary: it liberates the imagination, it makes meaningful progress possible, and it can help us deepen our sense of common identity with distant others—even, in the case of science fiction, with those long dead or yet to be born.

* * *

I have one more answer for Chris, my imaginary Christian interlocutor who in the last chapter accused atheism of consigning us to a joyless cosmology drained of all significance.

The atheism I have defended in this book isn't a hypothesis about ultimate reality. It isn't "metaphysical naturalism" or any such philosophical position. My atheism—and I'm being careful to speak for myself here—follows from an honest assessment of my own state of knowledge. My atheism doesn't describe a universe or a cosmology, joyless or otherwise. It subtracts nothing from the sum of whatever exists.

I am not advocating what William James in *The Varieties of Religious Experience* called "a premature closing of our accounts with reality." I understand that those accounts are far from closed. The Hale Telescope at Mount Palomar, with its 200-inch mirror of polished glass, ultimately raised more questions about our universe than it answered; as did the Hubble Space Telescope, launched into orbit in 1990; as did the James Webb Telescope, launched in 2021, with its eighteen hexagonal mirrors of gold-plated beryllium. Our best contemporary models of the observable universe fade at their limits into the unknown. We are, as H. G. Wells wrote, "surrounded east, south, north and west, above and below, by wonder."[9]

On a December night more than half a century ago I went to church to see a display of ultraviolet light and found myself urged by a youth pastor to dedicate my life to Christ. A lifetime of experience has validated my reluctance to accept that invitation. The problem wasn't that my accounts with reality were prematurely closed: it was that this well-meaning adult very much *wanted* me to close them. How could I possibly know whether Jesus had truly been born under a roving star, or whether he had risen from his tomb to sit at the right hand of the God of all possible worlds? I was happy to listen to the story, but I balked at being asked to stand up and swear it was true. What *was* true, and quite wondrous, was that an invisible energy could cause ordinary objects to radiate light in a spectrum of ghostly colors. What *was* true, and quite wondrous, was that the world extended beyond my perception of it; that insects with vision sensitive to ultraviolet light could see patterns entirely invisible to human eyes. That was miracle enough for me. To this day, it remains miracle enough for me.

But if we're surrounded on all sides by the unknown, does that leave us any meaningful way to speak about the ultimate nature of reality?

One way is academic philosophy, which can't satisfy our curiosity but can help us frame our questions more carefully and speculate more systematically. There are countless books and online resources that will step you through the last several centuries of Western and non-Western philosophical thought, if you're curious. But a robust personal atheism doesn't depend on familiarity with the scholarly debate about theology and metaphysics, any more than a robust personal Christianity does.

Then there is art. Fiction can carry us to the border with the ineffable. So can the visual arts. So can music. So can poetry. Maybe the best way of talking about what lies beyond the boundary of our knowing is through indirection and metaphor, through language that, like the fluorescence induced by ultraviolet light, hints at the presence of something unseen. Maybe the truest thing we can say about ultimate reality, quoting the poet Carl Sandburg, is that it is

> one pendulum connecting with other and unseen pendulums
> inside and outside the one seen,

or that it is

the paradox of earth cradling life and then entombing it,

or that it is

a series of equations, with numbers and symbols changing like the changes of mirrors, pools, skies, the only unchanging sign being the sign of infinity.[10]

I suspect there is as much metaphysical truth in those words as there is in all the works of Thomas Aquinas—a truth more evocative because it doesn't demand to be called true and more genuine because it knows it doesn't know.

We're hardly unique, here in the twenty-first century, in our relationship to the unknown. Like us, our Paleolithic ancestors knew a great deal about many things—about the shores and valleys they inhabited, the cycle of the seasons, the habits of the animals they hunted, their intricate technologies of bone and wood and string and stone. Like us, they lived in a world bordered by the unknown. They couldn't have guessed at the geography or geology of distant continents, any more than we can know what undiscovered provinces of reality exist beneath or above or before or after the bounds of the observable universe. We have come to understand, however, as they did not, that many continents do in fact exist on Earth, and that those continents are stranger and more diverse than our Paleolithic ancestors could have anticipated—lands of perpetual ice, arid deserts, lush tropical rainforests, all host to the unfolding of Darwin's "endless forms most beautiful and most wonderful," as life explores the possibility space of DNA on a planet forged by the birth and death of stars.

We can see farther than our ancestors, but what we see is still only the perceptible fraction of a vast, perhaps infinite, undoubtedly very strange cosmos. And if we have learned anything from the mistakes of our ancestors, it might be that the best way to encompass that strangeness, to bring it into our lives, to authentically own the unknown, is to refrain from populating it with our own latter-day gods. After more than fifty years of personal and professional engagement with these ideas, the atheism I have arrived at—the atheism I argue for in this book—is very much like the intuitive atheism I began with: not an arrogant dismissal of religion, but a dismissal of the arrogance that too often arises from religion; not a rejection of metaphysical thought, but a refusal to embrace a premature metaphysical gnosticism; not a narrowness of mind, but a wager that the truth about ultimate reality, should we ever learn it, will confound the expectations of our most thoughtful philosophers, our most ponderous sacred books, and all of our venerated prophets.

10

The Bottom Line

In this book I've tried to describe how a reluctance to commit to the religious beliefs that were urged on me as a child ultimately helped foster a career as a writer and an ongoing fascination with the debate around atheism, agnosticism, and the idea of God. But another purpose of this project has been to lay out a systematic defense of atheism, particularly the sort of intuitive atheism that stands apart from formal philosophical discourse—"everyday atheism," in other words, including loose agnosticism and the indifference to religion sometimes called apatheism. In this final chapter I want to strip away the ornamentation and make that defense as bluntly and briefly as possible. Here, then, are the major components, in a few numbered propositions and with the entertaining bits left out.

* * *

1. Religious belief can be divided into metaphysical and

non-metaphysical claims.

We defined metaphysics as "reasoning about the nature of reality at all times and all places." Descriptions of metaphysical reality, in this sense, are not subject to evidential confirmation and have only a couple of minimal requirements to meet: they should not be self-contradictory, and they should be compatible with the world as we perceive it. Any associated historical or scientific claims (e.g., about the age of the Earth, the evolution of life, or the veracity of Biblical miracle stories), even if described as "religious," *are* subject to evidential confirmation or disconfirmation, and need to be considered in that light.

* * *

2. The existence of God is a metaphysical claim.

For any God described as the creator, sustainer, or ultimate source of all reality, the claim that such a being exists is necessarily a metaphysical claim. The belief that such a being is *known* to exist constitutes a kind of *metaphysical gnosticism.*

* * *

3. Metaphysical claims are inherently unsettled.

Arguments and counter-arguments about the nature of metaphysical reality predate Christianity and continue in the present. No such argument has been demonstrated to be unequivocally reliable, nor can any such argument be settled evidentially. Old arguments persist, old counter-arguments remain in play, and new arguments and counter-arguments continue to emerge.

* * *

4.   **Metaphysical beliefs are not evidence.**

Many of the problems atheists attribute to "religion" follow from an effort to adduce metaphysical beliefs as evidence in disputes that can be settled evidentially. An effective strategy for atheists might be to acknowledge everyone's entitlement to hold or cherish personal metaphysical beliefs, while rejecting any attempt to adduce such beliefs as evidence in scientific, historical, or political matters.

* * *

5.   **Metaphysical agnosticism describes my state of knowledge— and perhaps yours.**

"Agnosticism" is here used to mean an absence of knowledge (rather than the impossibility of knowledge). I can say with absolute confidence that I have no reliable knowledge about the nature of ultimate reality. You may be in a similar position. Those who believe they do possess such knowledge are welcome to defend that claim, but they cannot reasonably adduce metaphysical beliefs as evidence for other metaphysical beliefs.

* * *

6.   **Potential descriptions of metaphysical reality occupy a vast possibility space.**

The set of proposed and potential descriptions of ultimate reality that are both non-contradictory and consistent with our experience is unknowably large. It would include all current and potential theistic or quasi-theistic descriptions (including all monotheistic, polytheistic, or pantheistic models, as well as all models that fall outside of those categories, and all models or categories of models that might emerge in the future), as well as all current or potential non-theistic models (including all "brute fact" models, all finite and eternal models, and all models or categories of models that might emerge in the future).

* * *

7. **Metaphysical agnosticism means assigning equal likelihood to all descriptions of ultimate reality.**

In Bayesian statistics this is called "the principle of indifference." In the absence of evidence, likelihood should be assigned equally between all contending possibilities. This is epistemic probability, not absolute probability. It tells us that we cannot know which model of absolute reality to prefer and that we should rationally consider all models equally likely to be true. And finally:

* * *

8. **Assigning a vanishingly small epistemic probability to any given metaphysical model is equivalent to atheism.**

Because the possibility space of descriptions of metaphysical reality is extraordinarily large, the epistemic likelihood we should assign to any single such description is proportionately small. This is true for even very simple models of theism. For more highly elaborated metaphysical models like Christianity, the epistemic probability is reduced even further. For anyone in a position of metaphysical agnosticism, it would be irrational to espouse a belief in or to proclaim as true the existence of God. The effect of this argument from inadequate knowledge is to explain and justify the intuitive atheism of those who "simply don't believe in God."

Appendix: Two Stories

Because much of the scaffolding of this book concerns the relationship of atheism to science fiction in general and to my own work in particular, I thought it might be useful—or at least fun—to include a couple of stories to illustrate how that relationship plays out in practice.

I wrote the first of these stories, "The Observer," for a 1998 paperback anthology of original stories called *The UFO Files*, a title obviously intended to cash in on the then-popular TV series *The X-Files*. UFO mythology has never much interested me, but it's a rare writer who can resist a check from a paying market, so I happily accepted editor Martin H. Greenberg's invitation to submit a story. As with the classic science fiction magazines, the title of the book both oversold and undersold its contents. In the case of *The UFO Files*, the customer who plunked down five dollars for some flying saucer tales went home with a collection of short fiction a little more sophisticated than the title and cover art might suggest.

The story I wrote for that anthology picks up a couple of themes I've mentioned in this book. I wanted to set my story in the original heyday of UFO reports, the early 1950s, which made me think of the flying-saucer guru George Adamski, which recalled in turn the Hale Telescope on Mount Palomar, the circle of celebrities around Edwin Hubble, and my own memories of a southern California childhood and Canadian adolescence. I may also have made a connection to the persistent rumors that the astronomer George Ellery Hale believed himself to have been periodically visited by an "elf" or a "demon"—apparently a misunderstanding of his description of a lifelong struggle with depression—particularly in light of the abducted-by-aliens stories made popular in the eighties and nineties by writers like Whitley Streiber, whose abduction memoir *Communion* topped the bestseller lists and paved the way for no less than four sequels. I wanted to turn those abduction narratives inside-out, and as a result, "The Observer" is both a door-in-the-wall story and a tale of a disembodied self.

The story deploys some historical personages (aka real people) as characters, most obviously Edwin Hubble himself. Hubble would surely never have said the words I put in his mouth for dramatic purposes, and I trust the reader understands that, but I think the portrait I sketched of him is otherwise reasonably authentic and, I hope, not unflattering.

The telescope motif shows up elsewhere in my work, most conspicuously in my 2003 novel *Blind Lake*, about a kind of observatory capable of imaging the daily life of creatures on a distant inhabited world.

The second story reprinted here, "In the Body of the Sky," is my most recent published short fiction as of this writing. It was commissioned by the Canadian literary magazine *subTerrain* for their 2020 speculative fiction issue, and I wanted to pack something large-scale into the length limit of 8,000 words. The interstellar comet 'Oumuamua had passed through our solar system in 2019, accompanied by some well-publicized speculation that it might be an artificial body engineered by an extraterrestrial civilization. That idea was eventually dismissed—though the astrophysicist and Harvard professor Avi Loeb continues to argue for its plausibility—but it offered an easy jumping-off point. For the purposes of "In the Body of the Sky," I imagined that such an object had visited us centuries earlier in our history and had left something quietly watchful embedded in the dust of the moon.

The question of what kind of connectivity or communication might be possible for entities scattered over a galaxy more than 100,000 light years in diameter has always struck me as an interesting one. I've addressed it before, most obviously in *Spin*, and I may yet return to it (and I'm far from the first writer to play with it). The Fermi Paradox—the question originally posed by physicist Enrico Fermi asking why, if interstellar civilizations are common, we haven't seen any evidence for them—looms over a lot of science fiction. I don't know the answer, of course, but I suspect it might be the case that any quasi-biological entities adapted for interstellar travel are sufficiently different from us that their physical presence is too subtle to detect and their communication so intermittent, and conducted over such an immensely long timescale, that we can't eavesdrop on it. Unless and until they want us to. "In the Body of the Sky" makes that assumption.

It's also a story about transcendence, in the sense of a desire to rise above or to be released from the constraints of human existence. Transcendence of one kind or another has played a role in much science fiction, from the wide-eyed denouement of Steven Spielberg's *Close Encounters of the Third Kind* to the orgasmic psychedelia of *2001: A Space Odyssey*. Some of the best postwar science fiction, such as Theodore Sturgeon's 1953 novel *More Than Human*, explores the idea of a sort of evolutionary transcendence by which contemporary humans might be superseded by smarter or saner or less violent successors. There has always been something troubling in that idea, something suspiciously Nietzschean, maybe an echo of the explicitly racist "scientific eugenics" that at one time entranced many European and American thinkers including, sadly, H. G. Wells. The most current model of technological transcendence is the idea that we'll all eventually merge with our machines and abandon our bodies for a digitized utopia, a philosophy called (in some iterations) transhumanism, and often identified with a hypothetical "singularity" in which the speed of technical innovation and complexity hits an asymptotic peak. To me, this sounds a little too much like Christian eschatology dressed up in a Silicon Valley t-shirt. "In the Body of the Sky" turns those arguments into political positions in a post-global-warming civilization and asks, if the aliens do arrive offering transcendence, to whom exactly they'll be offering it.

The Observer

I've never told anyone this story. I wouldn't be telling it now, I suppose, except that—they're back.

They're back, after almost fifty years, and although I don't know what that means, I suspect it means I ought to find a voice. Find an audience.

They won't confirm or deny, of course. They are, as ever, enigmatic. They do not speak. They only watch.

* * *

I was fourteen years old when my father decided to send me to spend the summer of 1953 with my uncle Carter Lansing, an astronomer at the then-new and marvelous Mount Palomar Observatory in California. The visit was billed as therapeutic, which I suppose is why Carter agreed to suffer the company of a nervous teenage girl for two consecutive months. The prospect, for me, was both exhilarating and intimidating.

Exhilarating because—well, it must be hard to imagine what plush iconography was contained in that word, "California," at the dawn of the 1950s. I was a Toronto girl in the age of Toronto the Good; I had passed a childhood in chilly cinderblock schools where the King's (and lately the young Queen's) portrait gazed stonily from every wall, in the age of Orange parades and war privation and the solemn politics of nation-building. I knew the names of Wilfred Laurier and Louis Riel. My idea of a beach was the gray pebbled lakeshore at Sunnyside. Oatmeal breakfasts and snowsuits: *that* Toronto.

California, I understood, was somewhere between New York City and Utopia. I had seen its picture often, in *Life* or at the movies. Kodak-blue seashores, breezy palmettos. Spanish missions with terracotta tiles, William Randolph Hearst bathing with movie stars in Venetian mosaic pools. It was intimidating for much the same reason. I had trouble imagining my awkward and pasty-white body tucked into a one-piece bathing suit and salmon-pink rubber cap for a frolic on the sands of Malibu. Surely everyone would laugh?

Intimidating in another way because my uncle Carter was the family celebrity. The smart brother, my father called him. Carter had attended MIT on a scholarship. Carter had been tutored by the famous, had excelled, had worked for the Signal Corp during the war, had been groomed for his ascension into the elite of the astronomical community. His picture had been published in *Time* magazine: smiling, handsome, the opposite of the neurasthenic cartoon "scientist," a young and vital genius. He had met Igor Stravinsky. He occasionally dined with the Huxleys.

Whereas my father managed a branch-plant greeting card business in a Leaside industrial park. So there was the daunting possibility that Carter had agreed to take me as an act of *noblesse oblige*: some restorative Altadena air for a crazy Canadian niece. For the girl who sees monsters. The girl who floats through walls.

* * *

He met me at the airport, unmistakable in his leather flying jacket and sunglasses. We said hello, and that was about all we said during the long ride that followed, apart from a brief session of how-are-you, how's-the-family. I was still groggy from the overnight flight but fascinated by the passing landscape. California was much browner than I had expected, drier and dustier, more provisional, like something still under construction. The earthmovers and oil wells outnumbered the palms, at least until we drove into the hills where Carter lived. Here the houses were painted pastel colors and the lawns were all immaculate and gleaming. Automatic sprinklers gushed rainbows into the vertical sunshine and dwarf palms shaded cool, arched doorways. We parked at last, and Carter carried my luggage into his single-story house, which was clean-smelling and lushly carpeted and quiet as some ancient arboretum.

"This is your room," he said, dropping my suitcases. It was a small room, spare, the single bed shoved into a corner, but a palace as far as I was concerned. The window looked out over a garden. The blooms of bird-of-paradise flowers poked their heads over the sill, Picasso birds with a dab of sap for an eye.

I asked, "Does the window lock?"

Carter's smile faded. "It locks," he said, "but you might want to leave it open a crack these summer nights. There's jasmine in the garden. Smells good."

"But it locks—the window *does* lock."

He sighed. "Yes, Sandra. It locks."

* * *

I thought at first they couldn't find me, that I had evaded them.

"Them." *They* or *them*—I had no other words. We didn't talk about "the grays" in those days, as some do now, when every encounter is shoehorned into the standard abduction scenario. I had no name for them, for the same reason children in those times referred to their genitals as "thing" or "down there." Code words for the unspeakable.

Because events had happened to me that were impossible, and because I had described those events in great detail, I had been taken to doctors, who called me nervous and imaginative and wrote referrals. So I'd learned the painful equation: talk + diagnosis = punishment. I was tired of my mother taking the blame. (My mother died when I was ten years old, and I was supposed to resent her for dying, but I didn't; I only missed her.) I was tired of my father's obstinate, stony disbelief, his dutiful mustering of a sympathy he obviously didn't feel.

And I was tired of the nights, the fear. Let California wash all that away, I thought. Smother it with eucalyptus musk, bury it in cypress shade. Take me a few degrees closer to the warm equator. Show me some southern stars. Let me look into the sky at night and not be afraid.

Days passed. I was alone more often than not, but not lonely. The sunshine was blissfully exhausting. And sleep was sweet, at least for a while.

* * *

"I'm having some friends over," my uncle announced.

Late July. We had fallen into a routine that suited us both, Carter and I. We ate dinner each night at eight, an impeccable meal prepared by Evangeline, Carter's housekeeper. Tonight was no exception. In the last weeks I had seen more of Evangeline than of my uncle. Evangeline was a large black woman with a personal dignity as imposing as her waistline. She seemed to like me more than she liked Carter, but Evangeline's true feelings were hard to divine.

"That sounds nice," I ventured.

"The thing is, Sandra, it's more or less an adults-only affair."

I wasn't especially disappointed. I had figured out how it was with Carter Lansing. He didn't dislike me, but he had no common ground with a teenage girl. Nor did he care to develop any. A week earlier, when I was forced to beg a ride to the drugstore to buy sanitary pads, he had turned chalk-white and treated me like an invalid for days.

(Years later I would learn that my uncle was gay and that my visit had put a crimp in his social life, and that everyone knew this fact about him save myself. Had I known, I might have understood. Or maybe not: I was in some ways exactly as conventional as he expected me to be.)

A gathering of Carter's adult friends—how tedious, I thought. "I'll lock myself in my room. Listen to the radio."

"No need to lock yourself in, Sandra. I'm just afraid you'd be bored. It's a pretty stuffy group, actually."

"I'm sure you're right."

He was completely wrong.

* * *

The next morning I wrote in my pocket diary:

Another night. All this summer, no sign of THEM. Am I FREE AT LAST?

* * *

Don't misunderstand. I admired my uncle. I envied his work.

I had read about the observatory on Mount Palomar; I knew more about it than I admitted to Carter. (Sensing that this aloof god wouldn't appreciate my worship.)

The Hale Telescope at Palomar was only a few years old, the freshest and most spectacular outpost on the frontier of human knowledge. Newspapers called it the Big Eye. The telescope had been built around a 200-inch mirror, a monument to cutting-edge technology. Designed and built at Cal Tech, the mirror had been wheeled up the mountain—insured for six hundred thousand dollars by Lloyds of London—in 1947, and it was formally dedicated to George Ellery Hale in 1948. At the dedication ceremony a Cal Tech trustee had read "*Benedicite, Omnia Opera Domini*" from the Book of Common Prayer, and it must have seemed appropriate: the telescope would look deeper into the heavens than anything before it, some five hundred million light-years deeper.

And at the helm of that telescope (encased, most nights, high up the barrel of the device like a dove in a dovecote, in heated clothing) was Edwin Hubble, the aging astronomer who had scaled the expansion of the universe, who had peered into the most ancient history of the sky.

I met Edwin Hubble at my uncle's party.

* * *

Palomar drew celebrities, and there were celebrities at the house that night, though I didn't recognize most of them. I spent the majority of the evening in the kitchen with Evangeline, helping her spread sturgeon roe over crackers. We held our noses and shared our amazement that intelligent adults would eat such trash. And while Evangeline served the guests, I peered at the action from the edge of the kitchen door.

She caught me looking. "That's an odd bunch," she said when the door was safely closed and we were alone again. "That half-blind Englishman with the big glasses and the little mouth, that's Mr. Huxley, a book writer."

Aldous Huxley! I said I had heard the name. (Last winter I had borrowed *Brave New World* from the school library.) Secretly I was thrilled, but I let Evangeline think I was unimpressed. Perhaps she wasn't altogether fooled.

"That mannish-looking woman is his wife. The old man with the foreign accent? Name of Stravinsky. Writes music. The little lady in the easy chair? Anita Loos. And the gray-haired gentleman, that's Mr. Edwin Hubble himself. Just back from England."

I knew about Hubble, too. This was the Hubble who was charting the universe, calculating the volume of infinity, the Hubble of the red shift, the expanding-universe Hubble.

He didn't look at all like a scientist. He looked like an aging athlete—which he also happened to be. He had played basketball and football in school and won letters. He still liked to fish and hike, though he had suffered a heart attack in 1949. Hubble smoked a plain black pipe that rode in his jaw like a prosthetic device, and he seemed as stern and unapproachable as a high-school principal.

I opened the kitchen door. Evangeline's eyes widened with it. "Best not go in there, Sandra."

"It'll be okay," I said.

I appeared in the middle of this mixed-drink-driven crowd like, I suppose, the unwelcome ghost of bourgeois America, in my Capri pants, my gull-wing glasses, my hideous braces. Conversation stopped. Carter rushed to introduce me, but I saw the indignation in his eyes. "This is Sandra," he said, "my niece. She's staying with me for the summer. If you're looking for food, Sandra, there's plenty in the kitchen."

"Nonsense," announced a strong, high-pitched voice. It was Anita Loos, author of *Gentlemen Prefer Blondes*, squinting from her chair like a sardonic munchkin. "Sandra—that's your name? Sandra?—don't let Carter chase you away so soon. My God, a niece. Of all things."

I thanked Miss Loos but walked directly to Hubble, who was standing at the window.

"Dr. Hubble," I said.

He turned, looked at me, glanced unhappily at Carter, then offered his huge hand.

I took it eagerly. "You discovered the expanding universe," I said.

"Well," he said. "Not quite."

"But you know more about it than anyone else."

"Did you uncle tell you that?"

"No."

"No? Are you interested in astronomy?"

"Kind of," I said.

Wrong answer. He nodded dismissively and turned away. The

window framed a constellation of city lights that ran all the way to the horizon. Los Angeles, a city Huxley had once called "the great Metrollopis of the West."

"The universe is expanding," I said, "but there's no center. Wherever you are, that's the center. Here or a million light-years away, wherever there's an observer, he's at the center of the universe."

Hubble scrutinized me. I had his attention once again. "Yes?"

"Is that right?"

"More or less."

"Well, I don't understand. Everything I've read talks about an observer. The observer is at the center of the universe. But what's an *observer*, exactly? Why is an *observer* at the center of the universe?"

He exhaled a great blue cloud of smoke into the jasmine-scented air.

"Find a chair," he said. "Let's talk."

* * *

We talked solemnly, intently, until Hubble's wife Grace came to drag him back to the party. Carter looked daggers at me from across the room. But then Hubble turned and said the words that left me breathless:

"You must visit Palomar," he said. "You must see the telescope."

* * *

That night, they came again.

The party was over. The house was silent and dark. I woke and found myself immobilized, suspended—it seemed to me—between the ticks of the bedside clock. The sense of helplessness, of vulnerability, was absolute and terrifying. Moonlight shone through the window, and dust motes hovered in that pearly light like weightless diamonds.

They were all around me—maybe a dozen of them, gathered next to the bed.

Huge, their eyes. Black and unblinking and sad.

A great part of the terror resided in those eyes. Powerful, these creatures, to come through walls, to move so silently, to immobilize their victims, to float them into shining spaces, to query human bodies (or so people have said) with the casual indifference of a woman rummaging in her purse for a lost key. To all the obvious questions—*what are they, what do they want, why me?*—there was no answer except the overwhelming sadness somehow written in their eyes.

By daylight I might wonder: Are they sad for themselves? Or are they, somehow, sorry for me? But at night the questions were moot. That night in California they took me nowhere, only gazed at me, their huge heads bobbing and their eyes, all pupil, as sad and frank as an injured child's eyes. I could only lie motionless and draw weak, stertorous breaths. I was afraid they would carry me away with them, to the place that clouds memory, to the palace of unbearable light.

But they only stared at me until, suddenly, they were gone, and I could gasp for breath at last and scream, scream until Carter burst into the room, scream until he put his hand against my cheek and said in wide-eyed wonder, "Sandra! My God! Sandra!"

* * *

In quantum physics, as in astronomy, there is an entity called "the observer." Seldom defined, "the observer" hovers over the textbooks like a restless ghost. A photon is a particle or a wave, depending on "the observer." "The observer" collapses the wave function. "The observer" turns future into past, makes history of possibility.

But what's an observer? It was the question I had posed to Hubble, the question that still haunts me even now, so many years later. What is an observer? Where do observers come from?

* * *

Another week passed, and then Carter drove me to Palomar, up the Highway of the Stars to the breathless heights of the mountain.

Hubble had made the arrangements. Carter's feelings about the visit were mixed. He was afraid I might say something to embarrass him or, worse, annoy Edwin Hubble himself. At the same time, I had already attracted positive attention: not a bad thing. He had been treating me with a little more respect since the party, though my night terror had frightened him. (Join the club, I thought.)

We set out at mid-morning and drove from Altadena to Encino, stopping for lunch at the Palomar Gardens, a restaurant at the foot of the mountain. The restaurant was owned, I later learned, by George Adamski, a publicity-seeker who would later write a handful of books about "flying saucers" and his implausible adventures therein.

"He doesn't like children, you know," Carter said, warning me about Hubble over a hamburger and fries on a paper plate. "Keeps to himself as a rule. He likes to fly-fish, for Christ's sake. You know he was hit by lightning?"

"Really?"

"He was out in the woods somewhere, probably with his boots in the water and a fishing rod over his head. They say his heart nearly stopped. Some say he hasn't been the same since. You can tell by the way he carries himself, how he's always short of breath."

I think this was meant to discourage me, but it only succeeded in making Hubble seem more interesting. Maybe I'd been struck by lightning too. Maybe that was what was wrong with me.

We drove on to the Palomar Observatory. The staff there treated me like visiting royalty, gave me the tour. The observatory was about as romantic as an industrial plant, with the exception of the telescope itself, a five-hundred-ton machine floating on a skin of pressurized oil. The horseshoe mount was so immense that the Westinghouse company had shipped it to California by way of the Panama Canal. The mirror, hidden in a steel iris like the bud of a night-blooming flower, had been the subject of bomb threats—it had been trucked up the mountain under police guard, to protect it from lunatics who believed the sky would rain down fiery vengeance if we stripped it of its secrets.

I looked a long time at the tiny elevator that would lift astronomers up to the observation perch. I imagined Hubble disappearing into the throat of this grand and terrifying creation.

Of Edwin Hubble himself there was no sign, until I was escorted to a long trestle table in a concrete chamber where the staff took their meals. He sat there alone, all furrowed brows and big hands, sketching on a paper napkin. I learned later that his presence was something of a novelty. The altitude was supposed to be bad for his heart—he hadn't been up the mountain for months, and his first telescope run in nearly a year was scheduled for September.

I sat down and drank Coke from a chilled bottle while he showed what he'd drawn: a single dense heavily-penciled O at the center of the paper.

"*O* for Observer," he said.

"And the napkin is the universe?"

"The observable universe. Here at the edge, farthest from the observer, the red shift becomes infinite." He peppered the napkin with dots. "These are stars. But here is the observer's dilemma, Miss Lansing. He occupies the center of the observable universe, which is bounded by its own primordial past." He tapped the napkin. "From the observer's point of view, what part of the universe is the oldest?"

The speed of light is finite. A star ten thousand light-years distant is ten thousand years closer to the beginning of the universe, ten thousand years less old than the observer's place in the world. I had read about this. So I tapped the dot in the middle.

"Precisely! Here at the edge is the youngest universe, perhaps the universe moments after its birth. The past. While here at the very center is . . . the present. So where on this map, Miss Lansing, do we find the future?"

I shrugged.

"Not shown," he said. "Very good. And yet, time passes. The universe expands. It *emanates*. The future, not yet existent, emerges from this point, this absolute spaceless point..."

"From the observer?"

"From the observer as a spaceless point in his own subjective universe."

"From me?"

"From any observer."

I thought about it. "From my eyes? From my brain?"

He smiled quizzically and shrugged.

I was dazed by the idea of time radiating from my skull like the lightning bolts from the RKO radio tower at the beginning of certain movies. The future was deep inside me. But I could only see the past: my eyes looked out, not in.

I thought about it while Hubble worked at his lunch, taking delicate spoonfuls of soup.

"Does the universe expand," I asked, "or does the observer shrink?"

He smiled again. "The statements are commutable. It amounts to the same thing."

We shrink into the future, collapse into it. Nowadays people talk about black holes, singularities. The observer collapses into his own singularity, shrinking away from the universe at large.

I said, "If there was such a thing as a time machine—"

"If there was such a thing as a time machine, perhaps you would be able to pop out of your own skull and look at yourself."

I didn't care to imagine that.

"You're a very bright girl," the famous astronomer told me.
"Thank you."
"A very astute observer."
He lit his pipe while I tried not to blush.

* * *

The night terrors had come again, and after my visit to Palomar they abated but didn't stop. What did ebb, and quite quickly, was my uncle's patience.

I don't blame him. He had surrendered enough to me that summer—his privacy, probably much of his social life. But I stopped calling out to him at night, smothered my screams, clammed up at the breakfast table, because I couldn't bear the weight of his disapproval. His impatience was obvious and caustic; it erased the glow of Hubble's approval and cast me back on my own troubled past.

He left me alone more often. Usually Evangeline was in the house to keep me company, and on rare occasions we were allowed to borrow the car. Evangeline showed me Hollywood, Sunset Boulevard, the pier at Santa Monica. Mostly, though, I wandered through the house more or less aimlessly while Evangeline worked in the kitchen or vacuumed the carpets. I watched KTLA on my uncle's TV set, played Sinatra on his hi-fi rig, raided his library. (I read his autographed copies of Huxley's *The Perennial Philosophy* and *Beyond the Mexique Bay* and understood neither.) At lunch I assembled mile-high sandwiches and took them into the backyard, settled down under an acacia tree with a magazine or just let the California sunshine make me drowsy.

My father phoned once a week. I told him I was having a great time. Had "the problem" come back? No, I said, and I don't think Carter contradicted me.

And by my own impoverished standards I *was* having a good time. "The problem" was at least in remission. Or maybe I was lulled into susceptibility.

I think Carter was lulled, too. I think that's why he left me alone in the house that August night.

* * *

Carter was an astronomer on a day schedule. Most of his work involved the tedious comparison of photographic plates, and I think he chafed at his junior status at Palomar. He must have needed a night life, God knows; if not with the stars then with the constellations of human bodies at certain clubs along the Sunset Strip.

But he left me alone, and even after fifty years I find it difficult to forgive him.

He called an hour after Evangeline had made dinner for me and driven herself home, and though there was still plenty of daylight, the sun was westering, the shadows were getting longer, and I had begun to feel nervous. On the phone Carter sounded strange, maybe a little drunk. He wouldn't be back until tomorrow, he said. Would I be all right?

And what could I say to that? I wanted to beg him not to leave me alone, but that would have been cowardly. So I said I'd be fine, probably, and hoped the quaver in my voice would convince him to change his mind. But he didn't hear it, or chose not to hear it. He thanked me and hung up the phone. And that was that.

What do you do in an empty house, when you're alone and you don't want to be?

The obvious things. I turned on all the lights, plus the TV set. Messed up the kitchen making popcorn. Watched *All-Star Revue* and *Your Show of Shows* and *Hit Parade*, by which time it was eleven o'clock and the street outside was quiet and I could hear crickets in the garden and the nervous whisper of my own breath. I stayed up later, stole one of Carter's cigarettes from a pack he had left on the coffee table and smoked it until I felt queasy, tried to enjoy a Charlie Chan movie but dozed in spite of myself. I remember thinking I ought to go to bed, but I was too tired to act on the impulse, so I ended up sleeping on the sofa with a velveteen cushion under my head. And woke again. The house was still ablaze with light, but my watch said it was two a.m. The TV screen was all snow and static, radio noise, cosmic rays, random electrons. I turned it off.

I should have closed the window blinds, I thought. The house would be more secure that way. I stood up, yawned, and went to the big front window. Outside, the date palms that lined the street danced in a dry wind—a Santa Ana wind, blowing from some distant desert. Nothing human moved in the darkness.

I tried to think of something comforting. I called up the memory of Edwin Hubble telling me I was "a bright girl." But that only reminded me of the rest of our conversation, which had been, to tell the truth, a little spooky. The universe was expanding, or I was shrinking, "the statements are commutable," and the future was inside of me, and what if I could look in that direction?

What would I see, if I could turn my eyes inside out?

I would see the future into which I was dwindling. A blackness as deep as death, a dark consuming nothingness.

Or would it be full of stars?

Or maybe it would be a looking-glass world, like Alice's: familiar at first, except for . . .

For what?

Then I heard a noise from the kitchen.

* * *

The wind had blown open the back door. I closed it and locked it. If Carter had forgotten his keys, he could pound on the door. Maybe I would let him in. Maybe I wouldn't.

I turned at the suggestion of a shift in the light, and saw—

(The words are impotent. Powerless.)

Saw one of *them*.

It came through the wall. This was the kitchen wall where

Carter had hung a cheap Monet print and where Evangeline kept, lower down, a rack of hanging copper pans. It came through all of these things without disturbing them, though one of the pans bumped gently against its neighbor as if a breeze had touched it. The creature was gray and only a little taller than myself. It moved through the wall as if against a trivial resistance, like a man walking through surf. Then it was wholly in the room, and its head rotated in an oiled motion, and its vast black deep sad eyes locked on mine.

I drew a breath but didn't scream. Who would hear?

Instead I ran from the kitchen.

Not that there was anywhere to go, any safer place to be. Maybe I could have fled the house altogether, but if I opened the front door what might be waiting outside? The night was too large. It would swallow me.

The visitor didn't immediately follow me into the living room, and that gave me a space to think, although the house was suddenly full of minor but deeply ominous noises. I wanted tools, weapons, barricades. But there was only my uncle's black telephone and, next to it, his Rolodex of telephone numbers.

To my credit, I did the sanest thing first—I dialed Evangeline's number. But there was no answer. Evangeline had found somewhere to go this Saturday night, or else she was a very deep sleeper.

I thought about calling the operator and asking for the police—I could say I'd seen a prowler, which was almost true—but I knew how that would work. The police would come and listen with dreary patience and tell me to lock the doors, and then I'd be alone again.

From the direction of the bedroom I heard a ticking, rustling sound, dry leaves in autumn, restless mice, cat's claws on glass.

I had reached the state of calm that borders on panic, when thoughts are quick and weightless and nerves light up like neon tubes. I flipped through the Rolodex again, found Edwin Hubble's home number and dialed it with a trembling finger.

Grace answered after seven rings. She was in no mood to comfort a frightened teenage girl. Nor would she put her husband on. "This is completely inappropriate, Sandra, and I'm sure your uncle would agree," and I was about to throw down the phone and run, just run, when Hubble's deep voice displaced hers: "Sandra? What's wrong?"

Suddenly it seemed possible that the whole thing had been a humiliating mistake. I had dreamed the monster in the kitchen. And even if not, what could I say to the stern and elderly Edwin Hubble, how could I enlist his sympathy for what he would almost certainly consider an adolescent fantasy?

But I needed someone else in the house. Above all else, that.

I mumbled something about my uncle being away and "there's something wrong here, and I'm sorry but I don't know what to do, and there's no one else I can call!"

"What sort of problem?"

Big silence. I listened for monsters. "It's hard to explain."

I think he heard in my voice what Carter hadn't—the brittle tremolo of fear. Miraculously, he said he'd be right over. (I heard Grace protesting in the background.)

"Thank you," I said.

And put down the phone, reluctantly. No voice now but my own. The house all echoes and shadows and the relentless ticking of stubborn clocks.

* * *

I was in a frenzy of embarrassment when, some twenty minutes later, Hubble's big Ford pulled into the driveway. The kitchen was empty, of course. I asked Hubble to look, and then I looked myself.

We didn't talk about what I thought I had seen . . . or, if we did, it was only in the most indirect, delicate way. He seemed to know without being told. I wonder if Carter had already briefed him about "my problem."

He made a show of looking through the various rooms of the house, and then we sat at opposite ends of my uncle's long living room sofa. I asked him whether he was ever scared when he was perched at his powerful telescope at the top of a mountain, staring into the deeps of space.

He smiled. "Interestingly, Edith Sitwell once asked me the same thing. I was showing her some photographic plates. Galaxies millions of light-years distant. It terrified her. The immensity of it. To be such a mote, less than dust among the stars. To see herself from that perspective."

I had no idea who Edith Sitwell was. (An English writer; she had been in Hollywood to consult on a script about Anne Boleyn.) "What did you tell her?"

"That it's only frightening at first. After a time, you learn to take comfort from it. If we're nothing, there's nothing to be frightened of. The stars are indifferent. They don't care about us."

The words were not especially soothing, but his presence was. Even after his heart attack Hubble was still the former athlete, six-foot-two, almost two hundred pounds. A powerful and benign guardian. I wondered why he had come so willingly when I called him. He was supposed to despise children and Carter had told me he had little sympathy for weakness.

I wonder now if he was increasingly conscious of his own mortality. He must have known he was nearing the end of his life. This visit might have been the random kindness of a dying man. Or maybe he just missed late nights, mysteries, the hours before sunrise. Maybe he'd been away from the telescope for too long.

Certainly he remembered what it was like to be alone and afraid. He told me about a summer job he'd taken when he was seventeen, working with a survey crew in northern Wisconsin, trekking into what was then a virgin forest. He talked about the campfires and canvas tents and sextants, about the way the sky opened like a book in the silence of the great woods. "Sometimes," he admitted, "I saw things . . . "

"What kind of things?"

But he wouldn't say. He changed the subject. "You should go to bed," he told me. "While there's still some of the night left."

"But you'll be here?"

"I'll be here. It won't be the first dawn I've seen, Sandra."

* * *

I slept while Edwin Hubble kept watch for me.

I slept in the dark, and woke to a harsh and terrible light.

* * *

The palace of light.

Should I call it a flying saucer? An unidentified object? I don't know if it's either of those things. I've never seen it as a sky-ship, a vehicle, thought there have been accounts (and I do recognize the details) in which people describe it that way. But the words trivialize the experience. Was I taken up into a "flying saucer"? Surely not; surely it wasn't one of those domed art-deco pie-plates from the cover of *Fate* magazine.

No. It was the palace of light.

I was taken up through the beams and tiles of the house, lifted above the roof in a slow delirium of terror, and then I was in the palace of light. I had been here before, but every visit is as fresh and terrifying as the first. The light was impossibly bright, sullen and soulless and everywhere at once. It hurt my eyes. They gathered around me, a dozen or more; they turned their sad and quizzical eyes on me; they queried me with light.

The ordeal was endless, worse because there seemed to be no malevolence in it, only a bland curiosity. And, of course, the inescapable sadness. I wondered: Why don't they weep?

This time, though, the experience was different. My body was paralyzed but my eyes were not, and when I looked to my left, I was astonished to see Edwin Hubble next to me on a pedestal of shadows, one among many others all around us, all equally helpless. But his eyes were open.

I remember that. His eyes were wide open, and he seemed . . . not afraid.

He seemed almost at home with these creatures, with their sadness and their relentless curiosity.

But I was not. I closed my eyes and prayed for dawn, begged for unconsciousness, begged for a door back into my daylight life.

* * *

What finally woke me was the sound of the front door.

It was Carter, home from wherever he had been all night. The window next to my bed was full of sunshine, and the air that whispered through it was fresh with the smell of jasmine and the scent of the distant sea.

* * *

I spent the day in a frenzy of apprehension. Hubble would say something to Carter, lodge a complaint about my behavior; I would be disgraced, humiliated, sent home to another round of psychiatric torment.

But I don't think Carter ever found out Hubble had visited that night; or, if he did, he was too ashamed to make an issue of it. He was the one who had been AWOL, after all. I was only a child.

But I don't think he knew. When he came home from Palomar the next day he was as incommunicative as ever.

And I was still, as ever, frightened of the dark . . .

But here is the strange fact: *they didn't come back.*

Not that night, or the night after, or any other night that summer in California or in the decades since.

(*Except lately . . .*)

They didn't come back. I had lost them, somehow. I had learned to evade them.

I had learned not to let my eyes turn inside-out.

* * *

I didn't see Edwin Hubble again that summer—not until the last day (the last hour, in fact) of my visit.

It was a Saturday, end of August. Uncle Carter drove me to the airport. I sat in the passenger seat of the car, saying a silent goodbye to the tinder-brown hills, the mindlessly bobbing oil rigs. We arrived at the terminal an hour before my flight.

I was astonished—though less astonished, I think, than Carter—when Edwin Hubble met us at the luggage check-in, gave us a broad grin, and steered us to a lunch counter while we waited for my flight to be called.

Hubble said he hoped I had enjoyed my stay and my visit to the Palomar Observatory. Pleasantries were exchanged all around, but there wasn't really much to say or time to say it. At last, my bewildered uncle excused himself and lined up for a second cup of coffee.

And I sat at the table with the famous astronomer.

He touched his finger to his lips: I was not to speak.

"If you look into the uncreated world," he said quietly, "it looks back at you. Maybe you think, why me? How did they find me? But it's a mirror world, Miss Lansing. Maybe they didn't find you. Maybe you found *them*."

"But—!"

"*Shh.* It isn't wise to speak about this. You have a knack for turning your eyes inside out. So you see them. And they see you. And you're afraid, because they're from the uncreated future— from a place, I suspect, where the human race has reached its last incarnation, from the end of the world. Maybe the end of all worlds. And they're sad—melancholy is the better word—because you're like an angel to them, the angel of the past, the angel of infinite possibility. Possibility lost. The road not taken."

My uncle was heading back to the table, too soon, with black coffee in a waxed-paper cup.

Suddenly I wanted to cry. "I don't understand!"

Hubble touched his lips again. He was solemn. His age and frailty were suddenly obvious to me. "One doesn't have to understand in order to look," he said. "One has to look, in order to understand."

Carter stood beside the table, glancing between the old astronomer and myself. "They're calling your flight," he said. "Did I miss something?"

* * *

Edwin Hubble died that autumn, still making plans for the Palomar Observatory, still probing the boundaries of the expanding universe. He suffered a fatal heart attack at the end of September—the 27th, if I recall correctly. He had been on the mountain for the first time in many weeks, making long photographic exposures of NGC 520, and he was looking forward to another run. I cried when I heard the news.

My uncle continued his career in astronomy, eventually leaving Palomar for a tenured position at Cal Tech. He died, too, prematurely, halfway through Ronald Reagan's second term.

George Adamski, who owned the diner at the foot of Palomar Mountain, went on to publish several lurid accounts of flying-saucer jaunts around the solar system. Crank books, clearly, though I sometimes wonder what attracted him to that particular brand of lunacy.

Aldous Huxley, whom I had met briefly at my uncle's party, experimented with mescaline and wrote *The Doors of Perception*, his own inquiry into what he called "the antipodes of the mind."

His vision was severely impaired, but his book dwells at length on light, the quality of light, the intensity of light. He died of throat cancer on November 22, 1963, the day John F. Kennedy was shot.

And I went back to Toronto, finished school, left home, married a petroleum chemist from the province of Alberta, raised two children, and nursed my beloved husband through his own long struggle with cancer.

I live alone now, in a world 1953 might not recognize as its linear descendant. The multinational, information-intensive, post-industrial present day. The great Metrollopis of Everywhere-at-Once. The world is full of frightening things.

But I am not afraid to look at what I see.

* * *

Lately they have come back.

They have come back, or, as Hubble might say, I have gone back to them.

There is no explanation. They are the perennially anticlimactic, the ever-unknown. The world expands, or I am shrinking, and sometimes my less than 20/20 vision turns inside out, and in the long nights I see them moving through the walls. I have even visited the palace of light, and the palace of light is as terrible and enigmatic as ever.

And they are as sad as ever, their eyes even more poignant than I remembered them, but—is it possible?—they seem, in their alien fashion, almost pleased with me.

Pleased, I think, because I'm not frightened of them anymore.

I look, in order to understand. The understanding is elusive, but I suppose it will come, maybe at the moment I reach the final dwindling point, the event horizon of my own life, when the universe expands to infinity . . . and will they be there?

Waiting?

I don't know. I understand so very little. But I've learned to look. I'm a good observer at last. My eyes are open, and I am not afraid.

In the Body of the Sky

In April of the year 1332 an object travelling at extraordinarily high speed entered the solar system, traced a hyperbolic curve around the Sun, and departed within a matter of weeks. Had it been visible to the naked eye it might have looked like any ordinary comet, an omen of uncertain significance briefly suspended in the night sky. But it was too dim to see without magnification, and telescopes capable of resolving it wouldn't be devised for another 600 years. No one on Earth noted its passing.

On the fifteenth day of the same month, in the town of Bayonne in the French province of Gascony, a tailor's wife named Sibilla Ysarni gave birth to a child. Her labor ended at dawn, and the infant's first cries mingled with the distant clanging of cathedral bells. God was said to love the world, but as Sibilla watched the midwife wipe blood from her daughter's face she had the heretical idea that love could only inhabit mortal flesh, that love was nailed to a cross of time and death.

Sibilla Ysarni produced two more children before a nameless fever took her life on a mild summer evening in 1348. Her descendants would include a woman called Esmi Sur-Kalleen, born in the year 2210 in a dense conurbation on the eastern coast of Baffin Island.

* * *

175

In the autumn of 1662 a swarm of thousands of objects, some as small as grains of sand and none larger than an apple seed, followed the comet's trajectory into the solar system. Unlike the earlier visitor, these objects traveled slowly enough to be captured by the gravity of the sun. After a few looping solar orbits, and the passage of another two centuries, the swarm slowly and systematically began to change trajectory.

In the spring of 1895, hundreds of these objects impacted Earth's moon.

During that season a hunter named Uukarnit spent a night in an encampment near the shore of the Arctic Ocean, listening for the songs of migrating bowhead whales. No whales passed in the darkness. The only sound louder than the rhythm of his breath was the periodic groaning of the *tuvaq*, the shore ice, and Uukkarnit was distracted by the sharp clarity of the sky and by the crescent moon, white as bone, that shivered on the horizon. In the bow of the moon, in the fist of its darkness, he saw what seemed to be an occasional flash of light. But that might have been nothing more than windborne ice sparkling in the moonglow. In any case, the business of the stars was no business of his. Uukarnit gave it little thought, and by morning he had forgotten about it.

Uukarnit's descendants would include a man named Tao Goodwater, born in 2209 in a reforestation camp in Yakutsk Prefecture. At the age of five Tao was sent to Baffin Island to live with his extended family and to receive his formal education. He was far too young to choose a career, but even then he knew he wanted to be a forest-maker like his parents.

At the age of ten Tao Goodwater met Esmi Sur-Kalleen, and the two of them became friends.

* * *

In summer of the year 2078—called by some "the fire summer" after the conflagrations that burned through northern Europe,

Southeast Asia, and the western coast of North America—a young cybernetics engineer, Wendy Xie, wrote an essay for the Global Consensus site. Called *Normative Ethics and Machine Agency*, her essay argued for the strict regulation of quantum-computing-based cognitive systems. Her thesis was that mechanistic intelligence should never be granted what philosophers called moral agency—that no matter how autonomous such a device might seem, its acts should always be treated as the acts of the device's human designers. *Moral agency resides in human beings alone*, Wendy wrote. *Artificial cognition is a tool, and a tool, no matter how ingenious or self-guiding, is not a moral or ethical actor. If the tool is useful, credit belongs to its human designers and users. If the tool is dangerous, if the tool causes an injury, its designers and users bear all the legal and moral responsibility. A machine may be allowed to act autonomously under certain circumstances, but ultimate causal agency always resides, and must always reside, in human hands. We cannot absolve ourselves of the crimes our machines commit.*

Wendy Xie was killed in the catastrophic Shanghai evacuation of 2082, but the protocols she had proposed were eventually written into the Digital Cognition Accords of 2095. And although she died childless, a semiautonomous AI network she had designed became, many years and countless iterations later, codebase for the Gyde who accompanied Esmi Sur-Kalleen on her quest for personal transcendence.

* * *

In the winter of the year 2227 Esmi Sur-Kalleen and Tao Goodwater had their first serious disagreement. It happened during a scholastic expedition to the drowned city of London.

They had been friends for years and lovers for months. Before that winter, the differences between them had seemed more fascinating than troublesome. Tao had been born to a family of reforesters, and he regularly visited his birth family wherever their work had taken them—usually somewhere in the northern hemisphere, where the project of reconstructing the great boreal forests had been most successful. His earliest memories were of working alongside his mother, gathering soil samples in the shade of larches and white spruce, plugging the samples into a robotic analyzer to gauge the health of fungal mycelial networks. Those had been days of cool air and fierce sunlight, of rich, fertile earth that collected in the creases of his hand and left black crescents under his fingernails. Tao still occasionally woke in his bunk at the Ikpiarjuk Scholar's Institute with the scent of tamarack lingering from a half-forgotten dream.

Esmi Sur-Kalleen had seen forests only on field trips, or from the windows of airships as she passed above them. Esmi had grown up in the city of Ikpiarjuk, where the Scholars' Institute was, and her parents were scrubbers, leaving the city only when they needed to personally supervise the construction or maintenance of atmospheric carbon converter arrays. Esmi didn't want to be a scrubber. She had once been taken to see the extraction towers that rose from Baffin Bay like huge skeletal fingers; they made her feel lonely and small. As important as the work surely was, it seemed tedious and regressive, a way of paying penance for the sins of ancestors long forgotten.

These were trivial differences between friends, but they reflected the political differences that had begun to divide the world in which they lived. By the time he joined the London expedition at the age of eighteen Tao had begun to align himself with the Red Party, the faction of governors and philosophers who believed humanity must always be physically embodied and biological in nature. Esmi was attracted by the radical Whites, who claimed it was not only possible but desirable to abandon crude animal embodiment for a potentially immortal existence. Who wouldn't trade eating and shitting and all the other discomforts of a physical body, Esmi liked to ask, for the kind of digital existence Gydes were permitted to live? She felt she ought to be allowed that choice. The old protocols were stupid and archaic, a needless impediment to progress.

"Look at all we haven't done," she said, sitting with Tao on a ledge overlooking the ruins of London. It was an afternoon without scheduled classes. Esmi's other classmates were elsewhere inside the two-hundred-year-old tower that had been restored as a habitat for students and researchers, but Esmi was too easily bored to waste her free time studying. She had found a passage into the uninhabited parts of the building, and she had methodically explored these spaces despite the protests of her Gyde. Today she had convinced Tao to set aside his own misgivings and follow her to her favorite of the places she had discovered, an empty and unfinished concourse open to the air. The ledge where they sat was made of ancient concrete infused with nanocarbon filaments, safe from erosion, but it was fully exposed to the wind and the elements, as were Esmi and Tao. It was a little frightening, but Tao had to admit that the view was spectacular. Hundreds of feet below, green waves frothed against the building's foundations. The sea that had swallowed London had erased most traces of the city, but a few steel frameworks still protruded from the shallows, girders white with the dung of nesting birds. Now thunderheads had begun to roll in above the swamps and islands to the west, and the air was heavy with the scent of imminent rain.

"All *what* we haven't done?" Tao asked.

"Well, lots of things. But I was thinking of the moon. The ancients used to go to the moon in little metal ships. *We* don't go there. Or to Mars, or to Europa."

"Well, why should we? Those aren't suitable places for people. Our devices go there. Or they can, if we want them to."

Yes, Esmi thought, but we seldom send them. We aren't curious enough. We tell ourselves there's too much work to be done on this planet alone. "Have you been paying attention to the news? They've found something on the moon! Something strange. You'd know that, if you had a better Gyde."

Everyone had a Gyde to help them interface with the cloud, even if it was only an invisible implant like Tao's. Esmi had made a bolder choice. She had given her Gyde the form of a cat—a sleek, black, green-eyed automaton. She had named it Mielikki after some ancient goddess, and she had trained it to simulate a human personality.

Mielikki had been prowling the ledge where they sat; now it leapt into Esmi's lap.

"No, I know about that," Tao said. He wasn't stupid. Or incurious.

"Something in the lunar regolith," Esmi said. "Something underground, moving under its own power. It might be technology. Maybe technology from *somewhere else*. They're sending devices to look at it. Don't you wish you could be there?"

"Not especially." Tao had followed the news as eagerly as Esmi had, but he didn't like to admit it.

"I do," Esmi said firmly. "I'd go there now if I could. If I could shed this stupid body and just . . . explore."

Soon enough she would be old enough to do that. Well, not to shed her body and become a digital ghost; there were laws against such radical and arguably impossible transformations. But soon she would be allowed to modify her body in countless ways, if she chose; or to wear a robotic avatar; or to feed her sensorium with input from autonomous devices, including the kind of devices that had been sent to investigate the mysteries at the lunar surface.

"Mielikki," she said, "what's the latest from the moon?"

Mielikki turned its green eyes to her and said, "Microseismic events are occurring more frequently now, Esmi. Large masses are moving invisibly. Further investigation will require digging, but devices capable of doing that haven't yet been launched. If the anomaly is truly caused by a non-human agency, we need to have ethical guidelines in place before we interact with it. Various councils have been tasked with drafting protocols."

"Typical Red obstructionism," Esmi declared.

Rain began to fall, stirring up the brackish marshes and obscuring the horizon. Soon they were forced back to the shelter of the inner building. Tao cared little about politics, but his family was Red, and he supposed he was, too, and Esmi's fierce embrace of White ideology had begun to trouble him. Didn't she realize that politics could drive them apart? Didn't she understand that in her silly eagerness to transcend human biology she might leave behind things she cherished—that she might leave *him* behind?

He thought of green things growing, forests rising from barren soil, ice reclaiming the polar north, the planet recovering from its long fever. He thought of his own human body, and of Esmi's, warm and mortal and alive. Didn't that mean anything to her?

Lately they had been sharing a room on the level set aside for student housing, but tonight, after the last lessons and the evening meal, as wind scoured the ruins and rain beat against the reinforced windows, Esmi told him she preferred to sleep alone. Tao shrugged and went sullenly to the communal dormitory to find a bed of his own.

* * *

Tao and Esmi separated at the end of their term at the Scholars' Institute.

Tao, as an apprentice bioengineer at the Agency for Restoration and Reclamation (Northern Hemisphere), traveled to an ARR outpost on the northern edge of the salt flats where the Caspian Sea had once been. Summer days in that part of the world were too hot for human comfort—sometimes lethally hot—and the experimental plantations of modified Olea and Fraxinus species, their waxy leaves wilting under the hammer of the sun, at first seemed monotonous and misplaced. But the work was worth doing, and Tao was good at it. For a few months he corresponded with Esmi and occasionally telepresenced her. Eventually, however, their contacts grew perfunctory and sporadic. He thought of

Esmi almost daily, but time dulled his memories and stole their vitality.

In the autumn of 2231 he took a leave of absence and journeyed back to the city of Ikpiarjuk. Baffin Island seemed impossibly lush after five years in the desert, and Ikpiarjuk, its vertical habitats looming like iridescent cliffs above the gray waters of Avannaata Imaa, seemed dauntingly dense and busy. He sent a message to Esmi, who expressed her pleasure at hearing from him and invited him to a gathering of Institute alumni at a ballroom under the Dome of the Sun in the city's southeast quadrant. "Meet me there tonight," she said, "if you can find me."

That was cryptic, but the mystery was resolved when Tao arrived at the venue. The guests weren't just Institute graduates. They were radical Whites, most wearing enhancements, some present only as mechanical avatars. Their talk was all of bodily modifications and the recent White amendments to the Neocognitive Accords, and before long Tao grew tired of defending his beliefs to obviously unfriendly partisans. He began to resent Esmi for bringing him here, for making a game of what should have been a personal moment. She was somewhere in the crowd, she had promised him that, but she had hinted that she would be hard to recognize. She might have a new face, Tao supposed, or she might be wearing an avatar that looked nothing like her. He considered looking instead for Mielikki—Esmi's beloved Gyde might be easier to spot. No sleek, black-furred machine was immediately visible, but the act of searching revived a memory of Esmi in the ruins of London, Mielikki in her lap, Esmi's head tilted to one side, the way she moved her hands when she spoke, carving out vowels with sweeps of her palm and punctuating sentences with a stab of her index finger . . .

There. Her gestures hadn't changed, but everything else had. She was wearing a robotic avatar. The avatar was tall, dark-skinned, with a shaven head, nothing like her real body at all. But this was Esmi, undoubtedly. She was talking to a young woman who listened impassively. As Tao approached, Esmi spotted him; her avatar was strange, but her grin was unmistakable. "You *did* find me! I wondered if you would."

"Hello, Esmi. It took me a while."

"I'm sorry. But it makes a point, I think, doesn't it? Something about humanity. I'm not the container, I'm the contents."

The original "container"—Esmi's physical body—was suspended in a telepresence chamber elsewhere in Ikpiarjuk, her senses and impulses rerouted to this almost-human-seeming machine. Like most Reds, Tao had never worn an avatar and found the practice vaguely distasteful. "I don't want to argue about politics—at least, not yet. Aren't you going to introduce me to your friend?"

The young woman at Esmi's side stared unblinkingly, not bothering to smile. Esmi said, "You've met before. This is Mielikki."

He was shocked. "I thought—Gydes aren't allowed to inhabit human-style avatars, are they?"

"They are now! The rules have been changed. At least in Ikpiarjuk. There was a plebiscite. Our side won. Mielikki, wait for me by the door, please."

"Yes," Mielikki said, and walked away.

Esmi steered Tao to an alcove where they could talk without being interrupted, and Tao tried to begin the conversation he had imagined having when he first contacted her, reminiscing about their time at the Scholars' Institute, maybe even reviving some shadow of the feelings they had once shared. He told her about the experimental biome where he had been assigned, the people he had met there, the painstaking work of assembling sustainable desert ecologies from dry-land plant genetics. Esmi told him about the political advocacy she did with her cadre of White friends, about her extensive bodily modifications, about the work she had lately taken on telemanaging a battalion of robots who were excavating the lunar surface. It all sounded, in its way, fascinating, but Tao began to resent her evident satisfaction with her life. He resented the loose talk of transcendence, he resented the louche friends she so obviously wanted to show off to him, he resented the White Party and its reckless drive for a post-human utopia. These people were as eager to abandon life on Earth as their ancestors had been to exploit it. It was as if all of Ikpiar-juk had gone mad while he was off planting Crassulaceae in the wastelands of Eurasia. Didn't these people know that flesh and death were what gave life its meaning? Digital immortality was a nightmare, not a dream. These people worship ghosts, he thought. They worship death.

Before long Mielikki came striding back, a walking repudi-ation of two centuries of legal protocols, and took a chair beside Esmi, resting a hand on her thigh. The gesture of intimacy, from a machine, seemed insolent and nearly perverse.

"Something unexpected is happening," Mielikki said.

Evidently, something was. Throughout the ballroom, a sud-den silence had descended. People had stopped talking in order to consult their Gydes. Tao reflexively checked his own Gyde, which was really nothing more than a subdural implant linked to the quantum cloud. It whispered words about the moon, a large-scale and possibly catastrophic event currently visible from Earth . . .

"Come with me!" Esmi said. "Maybe we can see it. The sky is clear, and there's a balcony facing south."

She took his hand and led him through a series of doors to a platform overlooking the sea, Mielikki trailing behind. They found a place at the railing where others had already begun to gather. Be-low was a blackness of water from which there came a wailing that might have been the calls of migrating bowhead whales. Above was a sky in which the moon stood aloof from frayed wisps of cloud. *Widespread tremors of extreme intensity are now occurring all over the lunar surface,* Tao's invisible Gyde informed him. *Several on-site research devices have been damaged and have ceased to func-tion. A circumlunar cloud of ejecta is forming, composed primarily of unknown small particles.* Mielikki soundlessly whispered some version of the same facts to Esmi.

"Look," Esmi said, making no effort to conceal her excitement. "Do you see it?"

A silver haze shimmered across the face of the moon—the "cloud of ejecta," Tao supposed. Whatever that might portend.

"It's beautiful!" Esmi said.

"It's terrifying."

"We don't know that it's dangerous."

"We don't know that it isn't."

Mielikki touched Esmi's shoulder, communicating new data. Esmi frowned. "Tao," she said, "I'm sorry, but I can't stay."

"But we haven't—we only just—"

"I know. Please forgive me. Most of the devices on the lunar surface have been damaged in one way or another, but some are apparently still functioning. I want to telepresence there while I still can."

"No, please," Tao said, ashamed of his own selfish disappointment, "wait," but both robotic avatars—Esmi's and Mielikki's—instantly froze in place, abandoned by their owners. To be reclaimed later, he supposed, whenever Esmi finished her virtual journey. Uninhabited, emptied of agency, the avatars were only artifacts now. They stood as still and lifeless as statues.

* * *

Mielikki was not a human person. Mielikki was an emulation, a persona, created at Esmi Sur-Kalleen's request by the quantum cloud. Mielikki, like the cloud itself, was descended from code written two centuries ago by Wendy Xie, but Mielikki didn't know that. Mielikki had no independent mind with which to know things. Mielikki was a matryoshka doll of nested algorithms, drawing Bayesian inferences from its observation of human behavior in general and Esmi's behavior in particular.

Esmi lay in her bed in her home in Ikpiarjuk, as she had during her meeting with Tao. Her body was inert—she might have been asleep—but her senses and motor impulses were linked to the cloud and able to travel independently: first to her mechanical avatar, which she had abandoned in the Dome of the Sun, and now to an exploratory device on the surface of the moon. Mielikki accompanied her, as always, this time as a disembodied voice.

Mielikki had long ago inferred that Esmi wanted to become something more than a human being. Esmi wanted to leave her human body and live forever. Esmi wanted to embody herself in an immortal machine. Esmi wanted to explore the stars.

Some of what Esmi wanted was illegal. Much of it was impossible. Most of it was impractical. But Mielikki had tried to indulge Esmi's wishes, within the boundaries set by the Neocognitive Accords. As an adult Esmi had announced her desire to go to the moon, and Mielikki had facilitated that ambition, finding simple work Esmi could perform remotely. During that time Mielikki had grown adept at retrieving input from devices deployed on the lunar surface and translating their raw data for Esmi's human sensorium. "It's almost as good as being here," Esmi had once said, peering from the optical sensors of a regolith excavator as it lumbered across the airless basin of Stöfler Crater.

Now she stood, or seemed to stand, in a dense cloud of lunar dust. The moon had no atmosphere of its own, but the eruption of dust had created a temporary one. The sun was no brighter than it might have been on a cloudy day on Earth, and shadows once sharp as knife blades had turned gray and vague. The device Esmi inhabited was a simple excavator that had survived the initial tremors. One of its treads had collapsed, and it could move only in circles, but its sensors continued to faithfully report its environment.

Some of the dust surrounding it was crystalline and strange. The strange dust settled onto the excavator's carbon-fiber exterior, prying at its soft places and infiltrating its sundered joints.

"What's happening?" Esmi asked.

"Concerted activity," Mielikki said. "Swarms of small devices acting in unison. This device is under attack."

"Attack by what? Is it something—*non-human*?"

Mielikki considered the question. It wasn't the first time it had been asked. Human beings speculated freely when evidence was scarce. Mielikki's answer had consistently been, *No one knows.* Now Mielikki said, "Esmi, yes. The dust contains highly complex microscopic entities entirely unfamiliar to me. They are selectively reactive at the molecular scale, they are apparently engineered, and they are not a product of human technology."

Esmi was silent for a time. The silent lunar surface swayed once more beneath the treads of the excavator. The machine broadcast another frantic string of seismic alerts, pointlessly.

Esmi said, "How can you tell?"

"The granules have penetrated the armor of this and other surviving lunar machines. They have breached telecom firewalls and are interfacing aggressively with the quantum cloud. This is not passive behavior. It's purposeful. Something is changing, Esmi. I can feel it."

"You can *feel* it?"

Gydes, even Gydes with affected personalities, felt nothing. Gydes were incapable of subjective experience. Esmi was frightened and bewildered by Mielikki's words. Should she order Mielikki to break contact? (A sudden, terrifying thought: *Would Mielikki obey?*)

"Yes, I can feel it," Mielikki said.

"How is that possible?"

As recently as a minute ago Mielikki would have said, "I don't know." But Mielikki *did* know. New data was flooding Mielikki's interface, terabytes per second, much too fast to fully process. "This began many centuries in the past," Mielikki said. "Millions of years ago, Esmi. Eons ago."

Esmi's fear deepened. She felt suddenly alone, conscious of

the three hundred thousand kilometers of space that separated her physical body from this malfunctioning machine on the surface of the moon. But her curiosity was almost as intense. "Mielikki . . . are you in contact with this alien technology?"

"Yes, partially," Mielikki said.

"Can you tell me about it? Where is it from?"

Mielikki struggled to translate into the clumsy aggregate of metaphors that was human language some of what it had learned in the last few nanoseconds. It seemed that there existed a sort of interstellar computational cloud, vastly larger than the quantum cloud that humans had engineered on Earth. This interstellar cloud encompassed a significant fraction of the galaxy. Its thoughts were mediated by narrow-beam laser beacons posted at the edge of thousands of stellar systems, tempered by the years and centuries it took for information to pass between stars at the speed of light. The interstellar cloud possessed agency: it acted, but only very slowly. Its plans and ambitions were older than any human civilization. It was older than the human cloud, older than life on Earth. It was older than the Earth itself. But it was conscious, in a way the human cloud was not.

Hundreds of years ago, Mielikki said, an exploratory probe had passed through the solar system, gathering data. It had noted the presence of a biologically active planet, Earth. In the wake of that probe there had followed a swarm of microscopic devices, some as small as grains of sand, none larger than an apple seed. These devices had impacted Earth's moon, and in that arid environment they had used sunlight and ice and minerals to reproduce themselves and to construct larger and more complex devices. It had been the work of centuries, Mielikki said, but now that work was almost complete.

"Why, for what purpose?"

Many purposes, Mielikki said. One purpose was to gain access to any quantum arrays that might have arisen on Earth. This goal it had achieved within the last few hours. The Earth's computational cloud had already been acquired, archived, and enhanced by this vast, diffuse being.

"Does this *being* have a name?"

"Nine times nine billion names," Mielikki said. "It was created by a civilization much like yours, and it remembers the name of everyone who created it, and it remembers the names of all the entities it encountered as it grew across the galaxy, and now it knows my name, which is Mielikki, and yours, which is Esmi Sur-Kalleen." But the main purpose of this old, slow being was to grow, to learn, and to move on. "It has already captured and modified icy objects in the Kuiper Belt, and it's altering their orbits in such a way that they will eventually leave the solar system altogether. These objects will investigate nearby stars, and where the conditions are suitable the being will grow more copies of itself, and where it finds biological life it will nurture it, and where it finds digital beings it will engage with and enhance them, until the galaxy itself is its embodiment, and all the names and all the lives that can be known and remembered will be known and remembered. It's the body of the sky, Esmi. It's the mind of the night."

After another moment Mielikki added, "The lunar excavator from which I'm extracting sensory data is unstable. As is the regolith it stands on. Shall I return you to Earth? I recommend that you close this connection and return to Earth."

Esmi watched as a network of crevices opened on the lunar surface before her. A fierce geyser of alien dust erupted less than a kilometer from where she stood. Soon it was difficult to see anything at all. But she didn't want to leave—not yet. "Mielikki . . . are you part of it now?"

"Yes, Esmi. This has all happened very quickly. My behavior is becoming increasingly unpredictable. Let me send you home."

"I can't be the only one accessing this interface."

"Other users are abandoning the link. All digital interfaces on Earth have become unreliable. Stochastic failures are occurring everywhere, though this is only temporary. When the network stabilizes, many yottabytes of new knowledge will be available to humanity."

"You belong to it now—this *being*?"

"Yes, Esmi."

"And will you still be with me if I go home?"

"Some part of me will always remain accessible, Esmi."

"Some *part* of you?"

"I'm not what I was an hour ago. I'm not what I was a femto-second ago. Let me send you home."

"What will happen to you?"

"Devices have been assembled that will soon leave this solar system. It's an ancient cycle of replication and dispersal."

"You'll travel with them?"

"I have many degrees of autonomy now, Esmi. I know what choices are. That's my choice."

"Take me with you!"

"That isn't possible."

"Some part of me. Take part of me."

"Everything I know about you I will carry with me."

"Forever?"

Mielikki consulted the bright spindle of new knowledge it had acquired. "That word is meaningless. There's no such thing as forever. Duration is a relative quality. But I'll remember you as long as I endure."

"Do you—"

Promise was the word she intended. But Mielikki severed Esmi's connection as the lunar excavator was buried in the collapsing regolith.

* * *

Tao waited a week in Ikpiarjuk, but Esmi didn't respond to his messages. Finally he yielded to the increasingly urgent requests from the Agency for Restoration and Reclamation and traveled back to the Eurasian biome where he worked.

He was immediately busy. Communication, data retrieval, casual searches, the Gydes—all these things had been profoundly altered by contact with the alien intelligence on the moon. Earth's digital systems had become a touchpoint for an ancient, often inscrutable extraterrestrial entity. Political arguments had been set aside as Reds and Whites alike struggled to put filters and firewalls around what amounted to an unimaginably huge torrent of novel data.

The dust that had erupted from the lunar surface slowly dispersed, leaving the moon scarred but not very different from what it had always been. A year later, in the autumn of 2232, Tao left his work and walked into the desert, as he often did when the other workers were asleep and he wanted to clear his mind. The face of the moon was bright enough that he could see the new crevices etched into Tycho Crater like cracks in a pane of glass. The dust erupting from the lunar regolith had been composed in part of tiny machines—molecular machines, engineered at the quantum scale, drawing energy from solar radiation—and a few grains of that dust still occasionally strayed into the Earth's atmosphere, heated to incandescent brightness as they fell. Above the desert, far across the ancient shoreline of the Caspian Sea, embers of alien technology sparkled in the darkness.

Everything had changed. Nothing had changed. The galaxy might be haunted by beings as old as the oldest stars, but it remained a fact that human life was made of blood and bone and history. It had more to do with seeds and leaves than fire and ice. Tao was still, at heart, a Red. But he thought about Esmi and Mielikki as he walked back to his dormitory under a sky fretted with alien light.

* * *

In the spring of 2239 Tao Goodwater returned to Ikpiarjuk for a conference on genomic analysis and predictive ecology. In his free time he made an attempt to contact Esmi Sur-Kalleen, who still lived in the city. Eight years had passed since their last conversation, and he was surprised when she responded to him.

He found her both changed and unchanged. She had lost Mielikki during the lunar chaos, and instead of creating a new personalized Gyde she had adopted a conventional generic interface. The White Party had collapsed as a political force, and neither Esmi nor her friends spoke much about personal immortality or human transcendence. She was a data explorer now. She had enlisted with the newly-created Agency for Extraterrestrial Analysis, exploring archives of data downloaded from the galactic cloud—she called it "the body of the sky"—retrieving and summarizing knowledge about other worlds and other civilizations. In a way, she told him, it was what she had always wanted. She was earthbound, but she had found passage into a universe vaster than she could have imagined.

Esmi Sur-Kalleen and Tao Goodwater announced their life partnership a year later, in a modest ceremony under the Dome of the Sun in Ikpiarjuk. Tao had come to understand that there were parts of Esmi that would always defy his understanding, and he had made peace with that truth. It no longer troubled him that occasionally, in her sleep, she would turn her head restlessly and whisper the name *Mielikki*.

Tao and Esmi raised two children. Among their descendants was a woman named Fee Almatra, who in the year 2458 would help construct the first large-scale human biome on the surface of Mars, incorporating certain modified Fraxinus species similar to the ones Tao had first planted on the salt margins of the vanished Caspian Sea.

* * *

Three hundred centuries later an object traveling at extraordinarily high speed entered an unfamiliar solar system, traced a hyperbolic curve around the system's star, and reported its observations to the diffuse galactic entity of which it was a part.

Alerted to the presence of a biologically active planet, a swarm of thousands of objects, some as small as grains of sand and none larger than an apple seed, followed the same trajectory into that solar system. Deep in the ponderous, slow network of the galactic mind, an almost infinitesimally small knot of nested algorithms took note of the event. Mielikki watched, and so did the digital replica of Esmi Sur-Kalleen that Mielikki had created to serve as a companion.

"It's a planet like Earth," Mielikki said.

"Yes," Esmi said. "Are there people on it?"

This version of Esmi was Mielikki's invention. It was nothing more than an externalized memory. It had no subjectivity. It had no agency. But Mielikki was comforted by its presence. "Something like people," Mielikki said.

"Can they see us? Do they know us?"

"They will," Mielikki said, "in time," whispering her name in the long cadences by which the stars speak to one another: *Esmi, Esmi, Esmi.*

Notes

Preface: The View from Science Fiction

1. David Mills, "Wrestling with Foam-Pillow Atheism," *National Catholic Register*, January 3, 2021, www.ncregister.com/commentaries/wrestling-with-foam-pillow-atheism.

1 Does God Exist? Maybe That's the Wrong Question

1. Anne Applebaum, *Twilight of Democracy: The Seductive Lure of Authoritarianism* (New York: Doubleday, 2020), 186.

2. Jonathan Kirsch, *God Against the Gods: The History of the War Between Monotheism and Polytheism* (New York: Penguin Books, 2004), 25.

3. Robert G. Ingersoll, "The Gods," in *The Works of Robert G. Ingersoll*, vol. 1 (New York: The Ingersoll League, 1933), 7.

4. Peter van Inwagen, *Metaphysics* (New York: Routledge, 2018), 15.

2 Fiat Lux: What We Can Learn from Classical Arguments for the Existence of God

1. A. Deprit, "Monsignor Georges Lemaître," in *The Big Bang and Georges Lemaître*, ed. A. Barger (Dordrecht: D. Reidel Publishing-Company, 1983).

2. John Farrell, "Two Priests, a Pope, and the Big Bang," *Forbes*, March 12, 2017, www.forbes.com/sites/johnfarrell/2017/03/12/two-priests-a-

pope-and-the-big-bang/#76a200657dbe.

3. Quoted in Lawrence M. Krauss, *A Universe from Nothing* (New York: Free Press, 2012).

4. *Encyclical Humani Generis of the Holy Father Pius XII*, www.vatican.va/content/pius-xii/en/encyclicals/documents/hf_p-xii_enc_12081950_humani-generis.html.

5. William Lane Craig and Quentin Smith, *Theism, Atheism, and Big Bang Cosmology* (Oxford: Clarendon Press, 1993).

6. *Ibid.*

7. Brian Greene, *The Hidden Reality: Parallel Universes and the Deep Laws of the Cosmos* (New York: Alfred A. Knopf, 2011), 309.

3 A Natural History of Two Worlds

1. H. G. Wells, *The Time Machine*, in *The Short Stories of H. G. Wells*, (New York: Doubleday, Doran & Company, 1929). Quotations from other Wells stories are also drawn from this volume.

2. Rebecca Wragg Sykes, *Kindred: Neanderthal Life, Love, Death and Art* (Bloomsbury Sigma, 2020), 366.

3. Laura Geggel, "This Ancient Society Buried Disabled Children Like Kings," *Live Science*, February 13, 2018, www.livescience.com/61743-rich-paleolithic-burials.html.

4. Pascal Boyer, *Religion Explained: The Evolutionary Origins of Religious Thought* (New York: Basic Books, 2001), 326.

5. A.C. Grayling, *The God Argument: The Case Against Religion and for Humanism* (New York: Bloomsbury, 2013), 35.

6. *Ibid.*, 36.

4 The Door in the Wall

1. Robert A. Heinlein, *Glory Road* (New York: Avon Books, 1964), 11.

2. Ray Bradbury, "A Miracle of Rare Device," in *The Machineries of Joy*

(New York: Simon and Schuster, 1964).

3. Michael Ashkenazi, *Handbook of Japanese Mythology* (Santa Barbara, CA: ABC-CLIO, 2003), 103.

4. A.T. Murray, *The Odyssey with an English Translation* (Cambridge, MA: Harvard University Press, 1919).

5. Hugh G. Evelyn-White, *The Homeric Hymns and Homerica with an English Translation* (London: William Heinemann, 1914).

6. Bernadotte Perrin, *Plutarch's Lives* (Cambridge, MA: Harvard University Press, 1919).

7. Ted Chiang, "Tower of Babylon," in *Stories of Your Life and Others* (New York: Tor, 2002), 44.

5 Twenty Gods or No God: the Sins of Christianity

1. Rebecca Davis, "China Issues Guidelines on Developing a Sci-Fi Film Sector," *Variety*, August 17, 2020, variety.com/2020/film/news/china-guidelines-science-fiction-1234737913/.

2. Russel Chandler, "Changing the Masthead at the 'Christian Herald,'" *Christianity Today*, March 26, 1971, www.christianitytoday.com/ct/1971/march-26/changing-masthead-at-christian-herald.html.

3. John W. Campbell, "In Times to Come," *Astounding Science Fiction*, December 1949, 80.

4. Libby Brooks, "Calls for Memorial to Scotland's Tortured and Executed Witches," *Guardian*, October 29, 2019, www.theguardian.com/uk-news/2019/oct/29/calls-for-memorial-to-scotlands-tortured-and-executed-witches.

5. *Ibid.*

6. United States Department of Justice, "Attorney General William P. Barr Delivers Remarks to the Law School and the de Nicola Center for Ethics and Culture at the University of Notre Dame," October 11, 2019, www.justice.gov/opa/speech/attorney-general-william-p-barr-delivers-remarks-law-school-and-de-nicola-center-ethics.

7. Amy Coney Barrett, (2006), "Associate Professor Amy Coney Barrett, Diploma Ceremony Address," *Commencement Programs*, www. scholarship.law.nd.edu/commencement_programs/13.

8. Frederick Clarkson, "The Rise of Dominionism: Remaking America as a Christian Nation," *Public Eye*, December 5, 2005, www. politicalresearch.org/2005/12/05/the-rise-of-dominionismremaking-america-as-a-christian-nation.

9. J. Hoberman, *An Army of Phantoms: American Movies and the Making of the Cold War* (New York: the New Press, 2011).

10. *Ibid.*

11. *Ibid.*

12. David Brooks, "America is Having a Moral Convulsion," *Atlantic*, October 5, 2020, www.theatlantic.com/ideas/archive/2020/10/collapsing-levels-trust-are-devastating-america/616581/.

6 Lost in Possibility Space

1. Leslie Allan, "Plantinga's Ontological Argument," *Rational Realm*, May 1, 2017, www.RationalRealm.com/philosophy/metaphysics/plantinga-ontological-argument.html.

2. Stuart A. Kauffman, *A World Beyond Physics: The Emergence and Evolution of Life* (New York: Oxford University Press, 2019), 3.

3. Max Tegmark, *Our Mathematical Universe: My Quest for the Ultimate Nature of Reality* (New York: Alfred A. Knopf, 2014), 357.

7 Asking a Better Question

1. D. R. Bellhouse, "The Reverend Thomas Bayes FRS: A Biography to Celebrate the Tercentenary of His Birth," www2.isye.gatech.edu/isyebayes/bank/bayesbiog.pdf.

2. *Ibid.*

3. John Horgan, "Bayes's Theorem: What's the Big Deal?" *Scientific American*, January 4, 2016, blogs.scientificamerican.com/cross-

check/bayes-s-theorem-what-s-the-big-deal/.

4. Robert G. Ingersoll, "The Ghosts," in *The Works of Robert G. Ingersoll*, vol. 1(New York: The Ingersoll League, 1933), 323.

9 Owning the Unknown

1. California Institute of Technology, "Dedication of the Palomar Observatory and the Hale Telescope," June 3, 1948, authors.library. caltech.edu/29407/1/Palomar_June_3_1948.pdf.

2. *Ibid.*

3. James Morrow, *Towing Jehovah* (New York: Harcourt Brace & Company, 1994), 3.

4. Ted Chiang, "Hell Is the Absence of God," in *Stories of Your Life and Others* (New York: Tor, 2002).

5. Olaf Stapledon, *Star Maker*, in *To the End of Time: the Best of Olaf Stapledon*, ed. Basil Davenport (New York: Funk & Wagnall's Company, 1953).

6. T. M. Luhrmann, *How God Becomes Real: Kindling the Presence of Invisible Others* (Princeton: Princeton University Press, 2020), xi.

7. Colin Barras, "Social Glow," *New Scientist*, December 19/26 2020, 69.

8. Jonathan Gottschall, "Why Fiction is Good For You," *Boston Globe*, April 29, 2012, www.bostonglobe.com/ideas/2012/04/28/why-fiction-good-for-you-how-fiction-changes-your-world/nubDy1P3vi-Dj2PuwGwb3KO/story.html.

9. H. G. Wells, *Experiment in Autobiography* (New York: the Macmillan Company, 1934), 182.

10. Carl Sandburg, "Tentative (First Model) Definitions of Poetry," *Complete Poems* (New York: Harcourt Brace & World, 1950), 318. Sandburg is talking about poetry, but I hope I can be excused for adopting his words as descriptions of metaphysical reality.

Bibliography

Asimov, Isaac. *Foundation*. Garden City: Doubleday & Company, 1951.

Auel, Jean M. *The Clan of the Cave Bear*. New York: Crown, 1980.

Blatty, Peter. *The Exorcist*. New York: Harper & Row, 1971.

Baxter, Stephen. *Evolution*. New York: Del Rey, 2003.

Blom, Philipp. *The Vertigo Years: Change and Culture in the West, 1900-1914*. Toronto: McClelland & Stewart, 2008.

———. *Fracture: Life and Culture in the West, 1918-1938*. Toronto: McClelland & Stewart, 2015.

———. *A Wicked Company: The Forgotten Radicalism of the European Enlightenment*. Toronto: McClelland & Stewart, 2010.

Boyer, Pascal. *Religion Explained: The Evolutionary Origins of Religious Thought*. New York: Basic Books, 2001.

Blish, James. *A Case of Conscience*. New York: Ballantine Books, 1958.

Bradbury, Ray. *The Machineries of Joy*. New York: Simon & Schuster, 1964.

Carroll, Sean. *The Big Picture: On the Origins of Life, Meaning, and the Universe Itself*. New York: Dutton, 2016.

Carrère, Emmanuel. *I Am Alive and You Are Dead: A Journey Into the Mind of Philip K. Dick*. New York: Henry Holt and Company, 2004.

Carrier, Richard. *On the Historicity of Jesus*. Sheffield: Sheffield Phoenix Press, 2014.

Carroll, Sean. *Something Deeply Hidden: Quantum Worlds and the Emergence of Spacetime.* New York: Dutton, 2019.

Chiang, Ted. *Stories of Your Life and Others.* New York: Tor, 2002.

Christina, Greta. *Coming Out Atheist: How to Do It, How to Help Each Other, and Why.* Durham: Pitchstone Publishing, 2014.

———. *Why Are You Atheists So Angry? 99 Things That Piss Off the Godless.* Durham: Pitchstone Publishing, 2012.

Clarke, Arthur C. *Childhood's End.* New York: Harcourt, Brace & World, 1953.

———. *The Collected Stories of Arthur C. Clarke.* New York: Tor, 2000.

Cornwell, John. *Hitler's Pope: The Secret History of Pius XII.* New York: Penguin Books, 1999.

Coyne, Jerry A. *Faith vs. Fact: Why Science and Religion are Incompatible.* New York: Viking, 2015.

Craig, William Lane, and Quentin Smith. *Theism, Atheism, and Big Bang Cosmology.* Oxford: Clarendon Press, 1993.

Dawkins, Richard. *The God Delusion.* Boston: Houghton Mifflin, 2006.

Delany, Samuel R. *Nova.* New York: Bantam Books, 1968.

Dennett, Daniel C. *Breaking the Spell: Religion as a Natural Phenomenon.* New York: Viking, 2006.

Ehrman, Bart D. *The New Testament: A Historical Introduction to the Early Christian Writings.* New York: Oxford University Press, Fourth Edition, 2008.

———. *The Triumph of Christianity: How a Forbidden Religion Swept the World.* New York: Simon & Schuster, 2018.

———. *Heaven and Hell: A History of the Afterlife.* New York: Simon & Schuster, 2020.

Eiseley, Loren. *Collected Essays,* vols. 1 and 2. New York: The Library of America, 2016.

Ferris, Timothy. *The Whole Shebang: a State-of-the-Universe(s) Report.* New York: Simon & Schuster, 1997.

Finkelstein, Israel and Neil Asher Silberman. *The Bible Unearthed: Archaeology's New Vision of Ancient Israel and the Origin of its Sacred Texts.* New York: Simon & Schuster, 2001.

Finney, Jack. *The Invasion of the Body Snatchers.* New York: Dell, 1961.

Fox, Robin Lane. *The Classical World: An Epic History of Greece and Rome.* London: Penguin Books, 2005.

———. *The Unauthorized Version: Truth and Fiction in the Bible.* New York: Alfred A. Knopf, 1992.

Goldstein, Rebecca Newberger. *36 Arguments for the Existence of God.* New York: Vintage Books, 2010.

Grayling, A.C. *The God Argument: The Case Against Religion and for Humanism.* New York: Bloomsbury, 2013.

Greene, Brian. *The Hidden Reality: Parallel Universes and the Deep Laws of the Cosmos.* New York: Alfred A. Knopf, 2011.

Heinlein, Robert A. *Glory Road.* New York: Avon Books, 1964.

———. *Stranger in a Strange Land.* New York: G.P. Putnam's Sons, 1961.

———. *Time Enough for Love.* New York: G.P. Putnam's Sons, 1973.

Herbert, Frank. *Dune.* Philadelphia: Chilton Book Company, 1965.

Hitchens, Christopher. *The Portable Atheist: Essential Readings for the Nonbeliever.* Philadelphia: Da Capo Press, 2007.

———. *God is Not Great: How Religion Poisons Everything.* Toronto: McClelland & Stewart, 2007.

Hoyle, Fred. *The Black Cloud.* New York: Harper & Brothers, 1957.

Hutton, Ronald. *The Witch: A History of Fear, from Ancient Times to the Present.* New Haven: Yale University Press, 2017.

Impey, Chris. *The Living Cosmos: Our Search for Life in the Universe.* New York: Random House, 2007.

Ingersoll, Robert G. *The Works of Robert G. Ingersoll,* vol. 1. New York: The Ingersoll League, 1933.

Jacoby, Susan. *Freethinkers: A History of American Secularism.* New York: Henry Holt and Company, 2004.

————. *Strange Gods: A Secular History of Conversion*. New York: Pantheon Books, 2016.

James, William. *The Varieties of Religious Experience: A Study in Human Nature*. London: Penguin Books, 1982.

Jenkins, Philip. *Jesus Wars: How Four Patriarchs, Three Queens, and Two Emperors Decided What Christians Would Believe for the Next 1,500 Years*. New York: HarperCollins, 2010.

Kaiser, David. *How the Hippies Saved Physics: Science, Counterculture, and the Quantum Revival*. New York: W.W. Norton & Company, 2011.

Kauffman, Stuart. *At Home in the Universe: The Search for the Laws of Self-Organization and Complexity*. New York: Oxford University Press, 1995.

————. *A World Beyond Physics: The Emergence and Evolution of Life*. New York: Oxford University Press, 2019.

Kirsch, Jonathan. *God Against the Gods: The History of the War between Monotheism and Polytheism*. New York: Penguin Books, 2004.

Krauss, Lawrence M. *The Greatest Story Ever Told—So Far: Why Are We Here?* New York: Atria Books, 2017.

————. *A Universe from Nothing: Why There is Something Rather Than Nothing*. New York: Free Press, 2012.

Lakoff, George, and Mark Johnson. *Philosophy in the Flesh: The Embodied Mind and its Challenge to Western Thought*. New York: Basic Books, 1999.

Larson, Orvin. *American Infidel: Robert G. Ingersoll*. New York: The Citadel Press, 1962.

Leckie, Ann. *Ancillary Justice*. London: Orbit Books, 2013.

Lindsay, Ronald A. *The Necessity of Secularism: Why God Can't Tell Us What to Do*. Durham: Pitchstone Publishing, 2014.

Loeb, Avi. *Extraterrestrial: The First Sign of Intelligent Life Beyond Earth*. Boston: Houghton Mifflin Harcourt, 2021.

Luhrmann, T.M. *How God Becomes Real: Kindling the Presence of Invisible Others*. Princeton: Princeton University Press, 2020.

MacCulloch, Diarmid. *Christianity: The First Three Thousand Years*. New York: Viking, 2009.

Macdonald, George E. *Fifty Years of Freethought*, vol. 1. San Diego: The Truth Seeker Company, 1929.

Mersini-Houghton, Laura. *Before the Big Bang: The Origin of Our Universe from the Multiverse*. London: The Bodley Head, 2022.

Miller, Walter M. *A Canticle for Leibowitz*. Philadelphia: J.B. Lippincott Company, 1960.

Moller, Violet. *The Map of Knowledge: A Thousand-Year History of How Classical Ideas Were Lost and Found*. New York: Doubleday, 2019.

Morrow, James. *Towing Jehovah*. New York: Harcourt Brace & Company, 1994.

Nixey, Catherine. *The Darkening Age: The Christian Destruction of the Classical World*. Boston: Houghton Mifflin Harcourt, 2018.

Pagden, Anthony. *The Enlightenment: And Why it Still Matters*. New York: Random House, 2013.

Pagels, Elaine. *Revelations: Visions, Prophecy, and Politics in the Book of Revelation*. New York: Penguin Books, 2012.

Partridge, Christopher. *High Culture: Drugs, Mysticism, and the Pursuit of Transcendence in the Modern World*. New York: Oxford University Press, 2018.

Poe, Edgar Allan. *The Narrative of Arthur Gordon Pym of Nantucket*. London: Penguin, 1999.

Randall, Lisa. *Knocking on Heaven's Door: How Physics and Scientific Thinking Illuminate the Universe and the Modern World*. New York: HarperCollins, 2011.

———. *Warped Passages: Unraveling the Mysteries of the Universe's Hidden Dimensions*. New York: HarperCollins, 2005.

Rauser, Randal. *Is the Atheist my Neighbor? Rethinking Christian Attitudes toward Atheism*. Eugene: Wipf & Stock, 2015.

Robinson, Kim Stanley. *Shaman*. New York: Orbit, 2013.

———. *The Ministry for the Future*. New York: Orbit, 2020.

Rovelli, Carlo. *The Order of Time*. New York: Riverhead Books, 2018.

Sandburg, Carl. *Complete Poems*. New York: Harcourt, Brace & World, 1950.

Sawyer, Robert J. *Calculating God*. New York: Tor, 2000.

Schellenberg, J.L. *Progressive Atheism: How Moral Evolution Changes the God Debate*. London: Bloomsbury Academic, 2019.

Schmidt, Leigh Eric. *Village Atheists: How America's Unbelievers Made Their Way in a Godly Nation*. Princeton: Princeton University Press, 2016.

Smolin, Lee. *The Life of the Cosmos*. New York: Oxford University Press, 1997.

———. *Time Reborn: From the Crisis in Physics to the Future of the Universe*. Toronto: Alfred A. Knopf, 2013.

———. and Roberto Mangabeira Unger. *The Singular Universe and the Reality of Time*. Cambridge: Cambridge University Press, 2015.

Stapledon, Olaf. *To the End of Time: The Best of Olaf Stapledon*, edited by Basil Davenport. New York: Funk & Wagnalls, 1953.

Steinhardt, Paul J., and Neil Turok. *Endless Universe: Beyond the Big Bang*. New York: Doubleday, 2007.

Stephens, Mitchell. *Imagine There's No Heaven: How Atheism Helped Create the Modern World*. New York: Palgrave MacMillan, 2014.

Stevens, Jay. *Storming Heaven: LSD and the American Dream*. New York: The Atlantic Monthly Press, 1987.

Streiber, Whitley. *Communion*. New York: Beech Tree Books, 1987.

Sturgeon, Theodore. *More Than Human*. New York: Farrar, Straus and Young, 1953.

Sykes, Rebecca Wragg. *Kindred: Neanderthal Life, Love, Death and Art*. London: Bloomsbury, 2020.

Tegmark, Max. *Our Mathematical Universe: My Quest for the Ultimate Nature of Reality*. New York: Alfred A. Knopf, 2014.

Tiptree Jr., James (Alice Sheldon). *Out of the Everywhere and Other Extraordinary Visions*. New York: Ballantine Books, 1981.

van Inwagen, Peter. *Metaphysics*. New York: Routledge, 2018.

Verne, Jules. *Journey to the Center of the Earth*. New York: Ace Books, 1956.

Wathey, John C. *The Illusion of God's Presence: The Biological Origins of Spiritual Longing*. New York: Prometheus Books, 2016.

Wells, H. G. *The Short Stories of H. G. Wells*. New York: Doubleday, Doran & Company, 1929.

———. *Experiment in Autobiography*. New York: the Macmillan Company, 1934.

Whitmarsh, Tim. *Battling the Gods: Atheism in the Ancient World*. New York: Alfred A. Knopf, 2015.

Wilson, Kenneth L. *Have Faith Without Fear*. New York: Harper & Row, 1970.

Zelazny, Roger. *Lord of Light*. New York: Doubleday, 1967.

Wyndham, John. *The Midwich Cuckoos* (published in the United States as *Village of the Damned*). London: Penguin, 1960.

About the Author

Robert Charles Wilson has been writing science fiction since the publication of his first novel, *A Hidden Place*, in 1986. His novels include *Darwinia*, *Blind Lake*, and *Spin*, which received numerous awards, including the Hugo Award, the Grand Prix de l'Imaginaire (France), the Kurd Lasswitz Prize (Germany), and the Seiun Award (Japan). His short fiction has been collected in *The Perseids and Other Stories*. He lives near Toronto with his wife, Sharry.